JJ Virgin's Easy, Low-Sugar, Allergy-Free Smoothies

30+ Delicious Recipes to Lose Weight and Feel Better Fast

JJ Virgin

JJ Virgin, CNS, CHFS, is the *New York Times* bestselling author of *The Virgin Diet, The Virgin Diet Cookbook,* and *The Sugar Impact Diet.* A celebrity fitness and nutrition expert, public speaker, and media personality, JJ Virgin is an internationally recognized expert in food intolerances, food sensitivities, and overcoming weight-loss resistance. She has appeared on *Dr. Oz,* Public Television, *Access Hollywood, The Rachael Ray Show, The Doctors* and *The Today Show* and blogs frequently for Huffington Post, Mind Body Green, and Prevention Magazine. She has been featured in *Women's World, Health, Los Angeles Times, In Style, First for Women* and *Cosmopolitan,* among many others.

Contents

WHY SMOOTHIES?

"If you could recommend just one simple change to your client for fat loss, what would it be?" an interviewer recently asked me.

She probably expected me to discuss food intolerances or suggest dumping added sugars. Maybe I would recommend burst training combined with weight resistance.

All those definitely contribute, but my number-one game changer for fast, lasting fat loss has nothing to do with exercise or changing what goes on to your plate.

I'm talking about a protein smoothie.

The whole thing takes *maybe* five minutes to prepare, provides all the nutrients you need to perform like a rock star, and keeps you full, focused, and burning fat for hours. I've had clients do nothing else but substitute one for breakfast and successfully ditch 5 to 20 stubborn pounds!

Studies confirm a liquid meal replacement "can safely and effectively produce significant sustainable weight loss and improve weight-related risk factors of disease."

Starting your day with a smoothie makes sense when you consider that breakfast sets your metabolic tone for the day. Convenient though they are, a sugary muffin or cereal will instigate a blood sugar spike-and-crash roller coaster ride, creating a cycle of hunger and cravings throughout the day that you can't get off.

A protein smoothie steadies blood sugar levels to keep hunger and cravings at bay. Studies show compared with high-carbohydrate foods like muffins and cereals, a high-protein breakfast reduces your hunger hormone ghrelin and increases your hunger-*suppressing* hormone cholecystokinin. Talk about a win-win!

"The last thing I feel like doing in the morning is eating a protein-rich meal," many folks confess. But a smoothie makes the perfect alternative whether you're traveling or juggling an especially hectic workday morning because:

It's simple.
Manufacturers know that between the frantic search for your keys and getting the kids ready for school, you're most likely to take the path of least resistance in the morning. A protein smoothie takes the guesswork out of breakfast. Just toss everything into your blender and in minutes you've got a portable grab-and-go meal.

It provides steady, sustained energy.
A low-fat muffin and large latte raises your insulin levels and jacks up your stress hormone cortisol, setting the stage for a late-morning crash that will leave you running for another sugary, caffeinated pick-me-up. A protein smoothie helps keep you focused with sustained energy for hours. That means no 11am doughnut cravings and no snapping at your co-workers once your blood sugar levels crash.

It's cost-effective.
Tally up how much you spend on bagels, coffee shop treats, or whatever else counts for breakfast. Surprised? For the price of a large coffee, you can throw together a filling, nutrient-rich, fat-burning protein smoothie.

It's fast.
You know that time excuse for not having breakfast? It doesn't work with a protein smoothie. In about the time it takes to pour cereal and milk, you can toss in and blend everything for a filling, delicious smoothie.

It's healthy.

Made correctly, a protein smoothie provides an excellent source of healthy fat, fiber, antioxidants, nutrients, and high quality protein.

WHAT TO LOOK FOR IN A PROTEIN POWDER

Protein sources There are two protein sources I prefer for shakes - pea and defatted beef protein. If you are a vegan or vegetarian look for a high quality pea protein, preferably in a blend with other plant sources of protein like chia, cranberry and/or chlorella. If you follow a more Paleo-inspired diet, look for defatted beef protein. It has the mouthfeel of dairy without the negative effects of it. Plus it is a great source of amino acids, easy to absorb and also provides collagen which is great for your bones, hair, skin and nails and supports the healing process. Avoid soy, egg, whey or milk protein powders.

Ideally, every serving will contain 20 – 25 grams of protein.

Go natural. Look for GMO-free and hormone-free (no recombinant bovine growth hormone, or rGBH).

Go low Sugar Impact. Look for 4–5 grams of sugar per serving, max. Less is best here so the closer to zero grams the better. Stick with a very small amount of natural sweetener or sugar alcohol (i.e., stevia, xylitol, erythritol, rice syrup, evaporated cane juice syrup, coconut sugar, glucose, dextrose). Avoid artificial colors or sweeteners and high Sugar Impact sweeteners such as fructose, agave, aspartame, and sucralose.

BASIC SMOOTHIE RECIPE

1 serving protein powder
1 serving fiber supplement
8-10 ounces liquid (water, unsweetened coconut, almond or cashew milk)
4-5 Ice cubes (more or less to your liking!)
Add-ins of your choice

FUN ADD-INS

Fruit – ½ to 1 cup
JJ Virgin's Extra Fiber – 1-2 scoops
JJ Virgin's Green Balance
Spinach leaves – 1-2 cups
Kale – 1-2 cups
Fresh ginger – 2 teaspoons or more to taste
Cinnamon – 1/8 teaspoon or more to taste
Vanilla extract* – 1/8 teaspoon or more to taste
Almond extract* – 1/8 teaspoon or more to taste
Peppermint extract* – 1/8 teaspoon or more to taste
Coconut extract* – 1/8 teaspoon or more to taste
Nutmeg – 1/8 teaspoon or more to taste
Coffee or espresso powder – 1 packet instant espresso, or ¼ cup strong brewed coffee (reduce your other liquid by this amount)
Cayenne or chipotle chili powder – scant pinch! Add more to taste
Avocado – ½ small
Raw cacao nibs – 1 tablespoon
Glutamine powder – 1 teaspoon
Nut butter (not peanut) – 1-2 tablespoons
Chia seeds – 1-2 tablespoons
Freshly ground flaxseed meal – 1-2 tablespoons
Hemp seeds – 1-2 tablespoons
Shredded unsweetened coconut – 1 tablespoon
Coconut butter – 1-2 tablespoons
MCT oil – 1-2 tablespoons

* no sugar added

LIKE THICKER SMOOTHIES?

Add more ice

Reduce liquid

Add chia seeds or freshly ground flaxseed meal

LIKE THINNER SMOOTHIES?

Reduce or eliminate ice

Add more liquid

SMOOTHIE RECIPES

ALL recipes are approved for The Virgin Diet and The Sugar Impact Diet Cycles 1 & 3.

Recipes that are also approved for The Sugar Impact Diet Cycle 2 will have this badge.

All recipes make 1 serving

Coco-Cashew Smoothie

The Sugar Impact Diet

1 serving chocolate protein powder
1 serving fiber blend
1 tablespoon freshly ground flaxseed
1 tablespoon cashew butter
8–10 ounces unsweetened coconut or cashew milk
5–6 ice cubes

Combine the protein powder, fiber, ground flax, cashew butter, coconut milk, and ice cubes. Mix on high until smooth. Thin with additional cold water if desired.

Peach-Berry-Almond Smoothie

The Virgin Diet Cookbook

1 serving vanilla protein powder
1 cup unsweetened almond milk (such as So Delicious Dairy Free)
1/2 cup frozen organic peaches
1/2 cup frozen organic blueberries
1 tablespoon almond butter
1 to 2 tablespoons freshly ground flax meal
1/4 teaspoon almond extract
1/4 to 1/2 cup cold water

Combine the protein powder, almond milk, peaches, blueberries, almond butter, flax, meal, almond extract and 1/4 cup water in a blender. Mix on high until smooth. Thin with additional cold water if desired.

Strawberry Protein "Milkshake"

The Virgin Diet Cookbook

1 serving vanilla protein powder
1 1/2 cups unsweetened coconut milk
1 cup frozen organic unsweetened strawberries
1 to 2 tablespoons chia seeds
1/2 teaspoon vanilla extract

Combine the protein powder, coconut milk, strawberries, chia seeds, and vanilla extract in a blender. Mix on high until smooth. Thin with additional cold water if desired.

Chocolate-Cherry-Chia Smoothie

The Virgin Diet Cookbook

1 serving chocolate protein powder
1 cup frozen organic unsweetened dark cherries
1 cup unsweetened almond milk
1 tablespoon almond butter
1 to 2 tablespoons chia seeds
1/4 to 1/2 cup cold water

Combine the protein powder, cherries, almond milk, almond butter, chia seeds, and 1/4 cup water in a blender. Mix on high until smooth. Thin with additional cold water if desired.

Mixed Berry and Avocado Protein Power

The Virgin Diet Cookbook

1 serving vanilla protein powder
1 cup unsweetened coconut milk
1 cup frozen organic mixed berries
1/2 small ripe avocado
1 to 2 tablespoons freshly ground flax meal
1/4 to 1/2 cup cold water

Combine the protein powder, coconut milk, mixed berries, avocado, flax meal, and 1/4 cup water. Mix on high until smooth. Thin with additional cold water if desired.

Peach Melba Smoothie

By Virgin Diet Community Member Tonia Murray

½ cup fresh or frozen raspberries
1 tablespoon unsweetened coconut milk
1/2 teaspoon Virgin Sprinkles
1 cup frozen peaches
1 serving vanilla protein powder
1 serving fiber blend
8-10 ounces ice cold water

In a small pan over low heat cook raspberries, coconut milk and Virgin Sprinkles until berries begin to break down and release their juices, creating a sauce.

Refrigerate the sauce for at least 30 minutes.

When ready to make smoothie, place the peaches, protein powder, fiber and water in a blender and puree until smooth.

Pour into glasses and stir in the chilled raspberry sauce.

50/50 Bar Smoothie

1 serving vanilla protein powder
1 serving fiber blend
8-10 ounces unsweetened coconut milk (such as So Delicious Dairy Free)
1 orange peeled
1 tablespoon freshly ground flaxseed meal
Ice to desired thickness

Blend all ingredients until smooth.

Strawberry-Chocolate Protein Smoothie

By Virgin Diet Community Member Gloria Philpott

1 cup unsweetened almond milk
1 cup strawberries
1 serving chocolate protein powder
1 tablespoon almond butter
1 tablespoon chia seeds
4 ice cubes

Blend all the ingredients in a blender, and process until smooth.
Note: if using frozen strawberries, you will not need to add ice
cubes.

Chocolate Orange Smoothie

---

1 serving chocolate protein powder
1 serving fiber blend
1 peeled orange – or 2 peeled tangerines
Dash of cinnamon
8-10 ounces unsweetened coconut milk (such as So Delicious Dairy Free)
4-5 ice cubes

Blend all ingredients until smooth.

Espresso-Almond Smoothie

The Sugar Impact Cookbook – May 2015

1 serving vanilla protein powder
1 serving fiber blend
1 shot espresso or 1/4 cup strong brewed coffee
1 tablespoon almond butter
2 teaspoons freshly ground flax seed
1/4 teaspoon almond extract
8-10 ounces unsweetened almond milk
5-6 ice cubes

Combine the protein powder, fiber blend, coffee, almond butter, flax seed, almond extract, almond milk, and ice cubes. Mix on high until smooth. Thin with additional cold water if desired.

High-Fiber Cappuccino Smoothie

1 serving vanilla protein powder
1 serving fiber blend
1 serving chia seeds
8-10 ounces of unsweetened coconut milk
Espresso powder (try a Starbucks VIA packet)
Dash of cinnamon
5-6 cubes of ice

Combine the protein powder, fiber blend, chia seeds, coffee, coconut milk, cinnamon, and ice cubes. Mix on high until smooth. Sprinkle top with a little additional cinnamon

Rise and Shine Mocha Espresso Smoothie

The Virgin Diet Cookbook

1 serving chocolate protein powder
1 cup unsweetened almond milk
1 tablespoon almond butter
1 to 2 tablespoons freshly ground flax meal
1 teaspoon instant espresso or coffee powder (or substitute ¼ cup strong coffee)
1/8 teaspoon ground cinnamon
1/4 teaspoon vanilla extract
1/4 cup cold water

Combine the protein powder, almond milk, almond butter, flax meal, espresso powder, cinnamon, vanilla extract and water in a blender. Add a few ice cubes before blending to make a thicker shake.

Mix on high until smooth. Thin with additional cold water if desired.

Nutty Chai Breakfast Blast Smoothie

The Virgin Diet Cookbook

1 serving Chai protein powder
1 cup unsweetened coconut milk
1 cup baby spinach
1/2 medium apple, peeled and cut into chunks
1 tablespoon cashew butter
1 to 2 tablespoons freshly ground flax meal
1/4 to 1/2 cup cold water

Combine the protein powder, coconut milk, spinach, apple, cashew butter, flax meal and 1/4 cup water in a blender. Mix on high until smooth. Thin with additional water if desired.

Turkish Coffee Chai Smoothie

Virgin Diet Community Member Christy Coutts Darden

1 serving Chai protein powder
5 ounces unsweetened coconut milk
5 ounces coffee
1 teaspoon chia seeds
1 tablespoon raw sunflower seeds
1/4-1/2 teaspoon cardamom

Blend all ingredients until smooth. Sprinkle additional cardamom on top for extra flavor.

Lean and Green Smoothie

The Sugar Impact Diet

1 serving vanilla protein powder
1 serving fiber blend
½ small avocado
2 cups baby spinach
1 tablespoon almond butter

1/8 teaspoon ground cinnamon
8–10 ounces unsweetened cashew milk (such as So Delicious Dairy Free)
5–6 ice cubes

Blend all ingredients until smooth.

Green Coconut Protein Smoothie

The Virgin Diet Cookbook

1 serving vanilla protein powder
1 cup unsweetened coconut milk
1 cup baby kale or baby spinach
1/4 small ripe avocado
1/4 medium apple, peeled and cut into chunks
2 teaspoons chia seeds
1/4 teaspoon coconut extract
1/4 to 1/2 cup cold water

Combine the protein powder, coconut milk, kale, avocado, apple, chia seeds, coconut extract and 1/4 cup water in a blender. Mix on high until smooth. Thin with additional cold water if desired.

Greens Apple Smoothie

1 serving vanilla protein powder
1 serving fiber blend
1 chopped apple

1 scoop of JJ Virgin Green Balance
10 ounces unsweetened coconut milk

Blend all ingredients until smooth. Add additional coconut milk if too thick.

Choco Chipotle Smoothie

---

1 serving chocolate protein powder
1 cup unsweetened almond milk
2 tablespoons almond butter
¼ teaspoon cinnamon
Scant 1/8 teaspoon powdered chipotle pepper (to taste!)
4-5 ice cubes

Blend all ingredients until smooth. Shave a few dark chocolate curls on top. (85% -100% dark chocolate)

Pumpkin Pie Protein Smoothie

Jeanne Peters, RD

½ cup unsweetened coconut milk
½ cup canned pumpkin
1 teaspoon pumpkin pie spice
1 teaspoon vanilla extract
1 serving vanilla protein powder
1 serving fiber blend

¼ cup cold water
about 3/4 cup crushed ice cubes or 8-10 ice cubes

Blend all ingredients in a blender – add more liquid, spices or ice to your desired taste and consistency.

This amount makes a pretty large smoothie - if you feel the need for an extra-large smoothie, this will do the trick.

Chocolate and Almond Smoothie

In the Kitchen with Leanne & JJ

Ingredients:
1/2 cup unsweetened almond milk
1/4 cup "Hint Water", flavor of your choice
2 tablespoons almond butter
1 serving chocolate protein powder
1 serving fiber blend
1 tablespoon cocoa nibs
4-5 ice cubes

In a blender, blend together all the ingredients until smooth. Serve right away.

Blueberry Ginger Surprise Smoothie

1 serving vanilla protein powder
½ cup frozen blueberries
2 teaspoons fresh ginger, finely chopped or grated
2 cups kale or spinach
1 cup unsweetened coconut milk
1 tablespoon chia seeds
4-5 ice cubes

This surprise is the fresh taste of ginger! Use a small piece of ginger, and use the back of a spoon to peel. Grate or finely chop the flesh.

In a blender, blend together all the ingredients until smooth.

Vanilla Pumpkin Spice Latte Smoothie

By Virgin Diet Community Member Caroline Drazin

1 serving vanilla protein powder
1/3 cup canned pumpkin
1 teaspoon pumpkin pie spice
1 Starbucks Via coffee powder packet
8-10 ounces unsweetened almond milk
5-6 ice cubes

In a blender, blend together all the ingredients until smooth.

Avo-Raspberry Cream Smoothie

---

1 serving vanilla protein powder
1 10-oz container So Delicious Culinary Coconut Milk (or substitute unsweetened coconut milk)
½ avocado
1 tablespoon chia seeds
1 cup frozen raspberries

In a blender, blend together all the ingredients until smooth.
Thin with filtered water if necessary

Mint Chocolate Crunch Smoothie

---

1 serving chocolate protein powder
1 serving fiber blend
10 fresh mint leaves, or substitute ¼ teaspoon pure peppermint
extract
8-10 ounces unsweetened coconut or almond milk
1 tablespoon raw cacao nibs

In a blender, blend together all the ingredients until smooth.
Top with additional cacao nibs.

Cherry Chia Almond Smoothie

1 serving vanilla protein powder
1 cup frozen organic unsweetened dark cherries
1 cup unsweetened almond milk
1 tablespoon almond butter
1 to 2 tablespoons chia seeds
4-5 ice cubes

In a blender, blend together all the ingredients until smooth.

Coconut Lime Smoothie

---

1 serving vanilla protein powder
1 serving fiber blend
8-10 ounces unsweetened coconut milk
½ avocado
1-2 cups spinach
1 tablespoon fresh lime juice
1 teaspoon lime zest

In a blender, blend together all the ingredients until smooth.

Berry Mint
Smoothie

1 serving vanilla protein powder
1 cup frozen mixed berries

10 fresh mint leaves, or substitute ¼ teaspoon pure peppermint extract

1 tablespoon chia seeds

8-10 ounces unsweetened coconut or almond milk

In a blender, blend together all the ingredients until smooth.

Lemon Cream with Sprinkles Smoothie

1 serving vanilla protein powder
1 serving fiber blend
1 tablespoon fresh lemon juice

1 teaspoon lemon zest
1 small container So Delicious Greek-style Cultured Coconut Milk plain, or substitute 8-10 ounces unsweetened coconut milk
4-5 ice cubes
Shake of Virgin Sprinkles

In a blender, blend together all the ingredients until smooth. Serve with a shake of Virgin Sprinkles on top

Kale Orange Mint Smoothie

1 serving vanilla protein powder

1-2 cups kale

1 orange, peeled

10 fresh mint leaves, or substitute ¼ teaspoon pure peppermint extract

8-10 ounces unsweetened almond milk

1 tablespoon freshly ground flax meal

4-5 ice cubes

In a blender, blend together all the ingredients until smooth.

Chocolate Blueberry Almond Smoothie

1 serving chocolate protein powder
1 serving fiber blend
1 cup frozen blueberries
1 tablespoon almond butter
8-10 ounces unsweetened almond milk
1 tablespoon raw cacao nibs

In a blender, blend together all the ingredients until smooth. Sprinkle some additional cacao nibs on top.

Honeydew Mint Chia Smoothie

1 serving vanilla protein powder
1 cup of honeydew melon chunks
small container of So Delicious Dairy Free Cultured Coconut
Milk, plain (or substitute 8 ounces of unsweetened coconut milk)
5 fresh mint leaves, or substitute 1/8 teaspoon pure peppermint
extract
1 tablespoon chia seeds

In a blender, blend together all the ingredients until smooth.
Thin with filtered water if necessary.

BONUS:
7-Day Virgin Cleanse

Welcome to my 7-Day Virgin Cleanse. With The Virgin Diet, I have helped hundreds of thousands of people identify the hidden food intolerances that have been holding their weight and their health hostage, and in my second *New York Times* bestselling Sugar Impact Diet, I have already helped thousands of people dramatically reduce the hidden sugars that have been sneaking into their diet and making them weigh more and feel worse than they should. This 7-Day Virgin Cleanse will show you how to remove hidden food intolerances and ditch sneaky sugars, so that you can eat the foods that are right for you and detox your body from the sugars and hidden toxins. In just 7 days, you will be lighter, healthier, and happier than you have been in years.

Within these pages you'll find a comprehensive, easy-to-use plan that helps you burn fat, ditch toxins, increase metabolism, and eliminate pesky symptoms that hold your weight and health hostage.

If you're doing everything correctly yet still struggle with weight loss resistance, toxic overload could be the culprit. Everything from the air you breathe to the water you drink constantly bombards your body with toxins. One study in the journal *Lancet* found among their repercussions, environmental toxins could trigger <u>fat gain and even diabetes</u>.

Toxicity's symptoms are often subtle. You might have a slightly lower-than-normal body temperature. Your doctor might find you have a normal thyroid-stimulating hormone (TSH) level but your T3 levels are chronically low. Sensitivity to smells, insulin resistance, and sex hormone imbalances can also signify a high toxic body burden.

You'll identify these and other problems with my **Symptoms Checklist**, which you'll take before starting and after completing my **7-Day Virgin Cleanse**.

Consider this book a reset button to reach fast, lasting fat loss, a newfound energy, and vibrant health as you reduce your toxic load in just seven days. In literally one week, my 7-Day Virgin Cleanse will transform you into a healthier, happier, less-toxic version of who you currently are.

<u>Why Do a Cleanse?</u>

Once upon a time, we lived in an unpolluted environment, drank pristine water, and ate whole, unprocessed foods that provided our bodies optimal nourishment. While not always a tranquil environment (those saber-tooth tigers could really ruin the day!), we didn't have modern-day incessant demands and low-grade nagging stress levels.

Things are different today. We live in a toxic world. "We are exposed to 6 million pounds of mercury and the 2.5 billion pounds other toxic chemicals each year," writes Dr. Mark Hyman. "Eighty thousand toxic chemicals have been released into our environment since the dawn of the industrial revolution, and very few have been tested for their long-term impact on human health. And let me tell you, the results aren't pretty for those that have been tested."

Among those not-so-pretty repercussions include poor digestion, low nutrient intake, lack of sleep, and chronically elevated stress-hormone levels. Even if you're eating an organic diet, managing stress, and drinking pure water, you can't escape toxins.

While we are all toxic, it really becomes a question of how high your toxic burden is and how much this is impacting your health. Toxic overload affects nearly *every* system and creates systemic hormonal imbalance.

Here's one example. Toxic overload makes your liver less able to handle those two glasses of pinot noir you had at the party.

Blood sugar imbalances impede your sleep, cranking up cortisol throughout the day.

Dehydrated, stressed, and slightly hung over, you reach for a big cup of coffee and an acetaminophen. A vicious cycle ensues as you become a wired and tired, stressed-out, toxic time bomb that's waiting to explode with your husband, kids, or boss.

All these repercussions take a big hit on your already-overtaxed liver.

On the Symptoms Checklist, you'll identify these and other issues that hold you back. As your body releases toxins, you'll notice your jeans fit a little looser, your symptoms don't feel so dramatic, and you have more energy and mental clarity.

How Detoxification Works

Most detoxification happens in your liver, which becomes ground zero to remove toxins. Essentially, everything passes through your liver.

Think about the Los Angeles freeway during rush hour. Toxic overload creates a similar traffic jam. During a cleanse, you provide the key nutrients to help unclog that jam so things can pass through more easily and your liver doesn't feel so overworked.

Your liver detoxifies in two phases. In phase 1, it converts fat-soluble toxins into water-soluble substances. In phase 2, your liver excretes these toxins via urine, sweat, and other bodily fluids. Without sufficient protein and nutrients, your liver can't perform that second phase, leaving highly toxic metabolites hanging around and wreaking havoc.

Put another way, an intelligently designed cleanse provides your body optimal nutrients that reduce toxic load and help your liver detoxify.

Why Most Cleanses Get it Wrong

Your best friend just bought a one-week detox kit from her local health food store, your sister raves about this lemon-juice-and-pepper cleanse, and your mom swears by a "colonic purging" she gets at her neighborhood spa.

Bring it up at your next brunch or dinner party and you'll quickly discover "detoxification" becomes a very broad term. Unfortunately, over the years I've learned most plans can actually make you *more* toxic. They leave you miserable, cranky, hungry, and craving those freshly baked double fudge brownies your coworker brought in.

Heavy in price but weak on science, here's why most cleanses get it entirely wrong.

They Do Not Focus on the Foods that are Right (or Wrong) For YOU!

They're High in Sugar, Especially Fructose

If you eat a whole apple, you'll get <u>about 23 grams of sugar</u>, but the five grams of fiber in that whole apple helps buffer out its sugar load, lowering its glycemic and fructose load.

Juicing strips away that fiber, surging your body with some nutrients but also copious sugar, mostly as fructose, the most metabolically damaging and liver-stressing sugar. You wouldn't eat four apples or oranges, but you could easily drink the equivalent in apple or orange juice. That fructose load adds up quickly.

Only your liver can metabolize fructose, and excessive amounts – easy to get on a juice cleanse – seriously increase its burden and take a huge hit on your health.

"Fructose causes insulin resistance and significantly raises triglycerides (a risk factor for heart disease)," <u>writes Dr. Jonny Bowden</u>. "It also increases fat around the middle which in turn puts you at greater risk for diabetes, heart disease and Metabolic

Syndrome (AKA pre-diabetes). And fructose has been linked to non-alcoholic, fatty-liver disease. Rats that were given high fructose diets developed a number of undesirable metabolic abnormalities including elevated triglycerides, weight gain and extra abdominal fat."

Think about it. When you cleanse, you want to reduce your liver's burden, but high-fructose juice cleanses actually create even more work for this overworked organ.

They're Low in Protein
Many plans also lack sufficient protein, which as I explained above jeopardizes phase 2 detoxification. Ironically, most commercial cleanses actually make you *more* toxic.

They're Low in Fiber
Fiber is another crucial component most cleanses overlook. Among fiber's many duties, it binds toxins that you then excrete. If you are not having at least one bowel movement daily, you are not completely detoxifying.

They Leave You Hungry and Miserable
Let's face it: most commercial cleanses are nothing more than semi-starvation diets. Dramatically curbing calories might initially create weight loss – not necessarily *fat* loss, since you'll be breaking down muscle too – but eventually your metabolism will come to a grinding halt as it compensates for this reduced load.

Is it really worth that Herculean effort when most commercial cleanses leave you cranky, miserable, hungry, and craving the donuts your coworker brought in? Add to that most people "break" cleanses with a gigantic high-sugar impact meal, reverting back to their old habits and frequently gaining back that weight and then some.

Why the 7-Day Virgin Cleanse is Different

Because most cleanses get it completely wrong yet so many clients asked for a comprehensive, easy-to-do cleanse, I designed my 7-Day Virgin Cleanse with a focus on:

1. **Eliminating food intolerances.** Gluten and other highly reactive foods can increase chronic inflammation, immune reactions, and leaky gut, all of which reduce your liver's ability to detoxify and force your body to hold on to that toxic load. On my 7-Day Virgin Cleanse, you will eliminate gluten, dairy, and other highly reactive foods that create these and other problems.

2. **Low-sugar impact foods.** Fructose particularly adds to our toxic burden because this particularly damaging sugar stresses out an already-overworked liver and exacerbates inflammation. Because your liver is detox ground zero, you don't want sugar (or *anything*) to add to that burden. My 7-Day Virgin Cleanse is low-sugar impact and low in fructose.

3. **Optimal protein.** My 7-Day Virgin Cleanse emphasizes clean, lean protein at every meal. You'll enjoy a delicious variety of protein smoothies as meal replacements, and your meals will include free-range poultry, grass-fed beef, and wild-caught fish.

4. **Nutrient-rich plant foods.** Tons of cruciferous veggies and other sulfur-rich foods are also on the menu. Sulfur plays a vital role in phase 2 detox, and on the 7-Day Virgin Cleanse you'll fill your plate with broccoli, Brussels sprouts, and cabbage. Sautee them in coconut oil to absorb their fat-soluble nutrients, and throw in some garlic and onions to increase your sulfur intake. You'll also regularly incorporate delicious,

easy-to-prepare Cleansing Green Soup to increase your nutrient intake.

5. **Fiber.** Detoxification begins with proper elimination. If you don't have regular bowel movements, you release toxins that are reabsorbed into your body, impairing digestion and exacerbating inflammation, food intolerances, and weight loss resistance. On my 7-Day Virgin Cleanse, I want you to gradually increase fiber until you hit a 50-gram daily quota to promote satiety but also regular bowel movements. That becomes easy when you eat raspberries, legumes, avocado, nuts and seeds, and other high-fiber foods.

Oh, and one added bonus you won't find in other cleanses: with a few caveats, you can keep your coffee. Yes, you read that correctly, and you can thank me tomorrow morning!

What Can I Expect During the 7-Day Virgin Cleanse?

Maybe you've never done cleanses before. More likely, past cleanses might have made you cranky, hungry, lethargic, and craving high-sugar impact foods.

Especially if you're incredibly toxic or consume a high-sugar impact diet, the first few days of my 7-Day Virgin Cleanse might be a bit challenging. That's not to say you'll feel awful or need to take a few days off work, but be patient with yourself and realize as you're healing your body, sometimes things feel a little worse before they become much better.

Most people find after pushing through the cleanse for a few days, they experience increased energy, healthier skin, better sleep, improved mental alertness, and – everyone's favorite – fast, lasting fat loss. You will also reduce or eliminate numerous symptoms that could hold your weight and health hostage, including digestive issues, constipation, and lethargy.

At the same time, I want to prepare you so you fully know what to expect during this cleanse. The three most frequent questions I get are:

1. "Will I be running to the bathroom all the time?" As your liver works to reduce toxic burden, you might find you're urinating more often or otherwise going to the bathroom more frequently. That doesn't mean you'll constantly be running to the bathroom, but be aware you might go more often and prepare accordingly.

2. "Am I going to feel like crap all the time while I'm doing it?" Especially during the first few days of cleansing, people sometimes experience a sort of crash that includes irritability, fatigue, and headaches. Sometimes symptoms become worse before they get better. You might become tempted to jump ship during this time, but stick with it and you'll discover a newfound vigor and energy.

3. "Will I be hungry all the time?" I mentioned you will never be hungry on this cleanse. My smoothies are incredibly satiating, and you'll find meals satisfying and filling. Remember thirst sometimes masquerades as hunger. See if a glass of filtered water doesn't curb your hunger before you reach for a low-sugar impact snack.

Let's Get Started!

I hope you're excited to look and feel better, eliminate symptoms that keep you from being your best self, and finally create fast, lasting fat loss. That transformation begins just one week from when you begin!

Throughout this book you'll find numerous recipes for delicious, easy-to-make, nutrient-dense smoothies here along with an intelligently designed meal plan and science-based strategies to effectively, effortlessly detoxify. Followed correctly, I promise you will *not* be hungry or miserable on this plan.

To prepare for this cleanse, I want you to use the shopping list so you're well stocked with essential foods for your success. I also want you to take the symptoms quiz to identify what could be keeping you tired, fat, unhealthy, and toxic.

Throughout these seven days you'll keep a daily journal. When I worked one-on-one with clients, I had one rule: they had to keep a journal. The reason is simple. Tracking keeps you on track, helps you identify any glitches that could stall your progress, and holds you accountable. One study in the *American Journal of Preventive Medicine* found those who wrote down everything they ate <u>lost twice as much weight as those who didn't</u>. Enough said, right?

At the end of your seven days, I want you to weigh again and re-take the symptoms quiz. Most clients see dramatic improvements and want to maintain this simple, effortless way to eat. You might also want to transition into The Virgin Diet or Sugar Impact Diet, based on your goals to reduce sugar impact or address food intolerances. I've provided a summary of each program so you get to determine your longer-term goals beyond the 7-Day Virgin Cleanse.

One final thing: doing this cleanse with a friend, coworker, or family member makes it more fun, creates additional accountability, and ups the ante for success.

If you want to take accountability and compliance to the next level, consider one of my <u>one-on-one coaches</u>, who work closely with me and can guide you through any glitches or obstacles that might arise during the 7-Day Virgin Cleanse.

Here's to your success!

JJ

Blueprint

- Prepare your Shopping List and stock your kitchen for your 7-Day Virgin Cleanse Meal Plan – Make a batch of Cleansing Green Soup

- Do the Symptoms Checklist

- Take your weight and measurements

- DAY 1 Journal page - Record your starting weight and measurements

- Record your daily water and fluids intake along with your meals for the next 7 days

- Day 8 - Record your weight and measurements

- Day 8 - Re-do the Symptoms Checklist

Regularity

Fiber becomes your secret weapon for fast, lasting fat loss, but let's be honest: Most of us think of fiber in terms of staying regular, or as I more irreverently say, giving you poops to be proud of.

Let's talk about poop for a minute. You need to have one to three bowel movements a day. They shouldn't be urgent, and you shouldn't have to run to the bathroom every time you eat, but you should be having them.

Fiber is your golden ticket for staying regular. When you work your way up to 50 grams of fiber daily, you can kiss constipation and other bathroom miseries goodbye. I say "work up to" because adding too much at once can create more problems. Instead, add five grams each day until you reach your goal, and make sure to drink more water as you do so.

A shake provides the easiest way to meet your fiber quota. Let's look at how you can step up your fiber intake with a fast, filling protein shake:

- 2 scoops plant-based All-in-One Powder – 6 grams fiber
- 1 cup raspberries – 8 grams fiber
- 1 cup kale – 3 grams fiber
- 2 tablespoons freshly ground flax seeds – 4 grams fiber
- ½ small avocado – 5 grams fiber
- 1 cup coconut milk – 1 gram fiber

Even without those berries, you get a whopping 19 grams of fiber in this shake!

You'll also want to work in high-fiber foods at every meal. Fortunately, a ton of low-sugar impact foods are loaded with fiber. My favorites include:

1. Berries – 1 cup raspberries has 8 grams of fiber
2. Lentils – 1 cup has 16 grams of fiber
3. Nuts – ¼ cup almonds has 4 grams of fiber
4. 1 ounce raw cacao nibs – 9 grams

5.   1 T chia seeds - 5 grams
6.   Quinoa – 1 cup has 5 grams of fiber
7.   Avocado – 1 cup has 10 grams of fiber
8.   Broccoli – 1 cup has 5 grams of fiber
9.   Artichoke – 1 medium has 10 grams of fiber
10. Other legumes – most beans have 13 – 15 grams of fiber per cup

Sometimes you're doing everything correctly, yet meeting your fiber quota becomes a challenge. You know what I'm talking about. You're at the airport, or stranded at your in-laws, and high-fiber foods are just not prevalent.

That's why I always keep <u>Extra Fiber</u> nearby. Every serving provides four grams of high-quality fiber from 12 sources. Extra Fiber is the Rolls Royce of fiber products! Another way to meet that quota is with <u>Green Balance</u>. Every serving combines six grams of fiber with a proprietary, high-ORAC greens, vegetables, and fruits blend.

Other ways to promote regularity include water, which along with fiber makes a nice sponge that will give the bulk you need in your stools. See below for instructions about drinking sufficient amounts of water.

A few supplements can also "help move things along." They include:

- **Vitamin C:** Start with 1 gram and increase as needed up to 5 grams each night.
- **Magnesium:** Start with 300 milligrams and increase as needed up to 1,000 milligrams each night.

If your poops become runny, back off the supplements a bit. Iron and calcium are constipating, so if you are taking either of these, you may need some supplements to offset those effects. I like to take vitamin C and magnesium at night to get things moving in the morning.

Some other ideas to improve regularity:

- Get things moving with exercise.
- Try drinking some hot coffee or tea in the morning.
- Sip some peppermint tea throughout the day.
- Throw two or three prunes into your shake.
- When you move your bowels, consider elevating your feet with a footstool. Our toilets are just about the worst possible setup for elimination.

If none of this is working, try cascara sagrada, senna, Chinese rhubarb and/or frangula (I prefer to use herbal blends of these) on a short-term basis. These are also great to take along if you happen to get constipated while traveling. You should only use them for a few days. Don't become dependent on them, as they may irritate the gastrointestinal lining long term with chronic use.

Note too that constipation and other bathroom problems can be a symptom of a more serious problem like thyroid imbalances. If you're doing all these things and nothing is happening "down there," please visit your doctor or an integrative specialist.

Water: The One Essential for Detoxification, Fat Loss & More

Listen, I know water is not the most exciting topic, but for fat loss, detoxification, and optimal health, no other substance proves more important.

Whereas your body should be about 70% water, dehydration can drop that number to 40 – 50%. As a result, your metabolism comes to a grinding halt and you increase your body's inflammation levels, frequently resulting in weight loss resistance and toxic buildup.

By the time you realize you're thirsty, you're already dehydrated. The trick, then, is to sip water throughout your day so you never reach that dehydration point.

Rather than buy expensive designer water in plastic bottles, I want you to carry a reusable bottle and keep it full. Whether at your office or gym water cooler, you have several opportunities to fill up your bottle throughout the day.

If regular filtered water doesn't thrill you, try sparkling water in glass bottles with a little lime. I love spa water with cucumbers, oranges, lemon, lime, and maybe a little mint or basil. You should also put a water filter on every tap in your home and track your water intake in your food journal. Remember that what you track, you can improve.

Here is the water schedule I recommend you adhere to:

- Within 30 minutes of waking up: 16 ounces
- 30 to 60 minutes before each meal: 16 ounces
- During a meal: limit to 4 to 8 ounces.
- Start drinking water again 60 minutes after each meal.
- Before bed: 8 ounces

The only time I *don't* want you drinking is during meals, when too much water can dilute stomach enzymes that break down protein. Otherwise, drink up!

Detoxifying with Lemon-AID

While you're detoxifying, I also want you to daily incorporate my delicious Lemon-AID recipe. This will count towards your daily water quota:

- Juice and zest of one lemon (or lime)
- 32 ounces water
- 1 teaspoon glutamine powder
- Stevia, monk fruit, xylitol, eryrthritol or Virgin Sprinkles as needed (use as little as possible)
- ½ thinly sliced lemon
- 1 tablespoon of chia seeds OR 1 serving Extra Fiber

Combine the juice and zest of one lemon with the water. Add the glutamine powder and sweetener (only if needed). Stir well and gently stir in lemon slices.

You might also want to drink fermented coconut water. Kevita or Coco-Biotic (see Resources) are my favorite brands.

No alcohol during this 7 Day Cleanse.

How Much Water Should I Drink Daily?

There are no hard and fast rules about how much water you should drink, and I hear people say there's no science to support the 64-ounce minimum.

Here's the deal. We don't need double-blind, placebo-based studies to verify water is crucial for good health. We know how important it is. So ignore the naysayers and drink *at least* 64 ounces a day. If you're heavier, live in a hot climate, or exercise rigorously, you need to increase that amount.

Ideally, you should be drinking approximately half your weight in ounces. So if you weigh 150 pounds that would be 75 ounces a day. However, this equation doesn't work once you get outside of the normal weight range.

The Institute of Medicine (IOM) report did not specify requirements for water, but made general fluid intake recommendations based on survey data of 91 ounces (that's 11-plus cups a day) for women and 125 ounces (15-plus cups a day) for men.

Remember, these guidelines are for *total* fluid intake, including fluid from all food and beverages.

Approximately 80% of our water intake comes from drinking water and other beverages, and the other 20% comes from food such as fruits and veggies, which are mostly water.

Assuming these percentages are accurate for most of us, the recommended amount of beverages, including water, would be approximately 9 cups for women and 12.5 cups for men. Exercise, pregnancy/breast feeding, and high altitude can all increase these needs by 1-3 cups.

7 Reasons Water is *That* Important

Whether you want to burn fat, build muscle, detoxify, or have glowing skin, here are 7 reasons that drinking enough water is *that* important:

1. **Water helps you eat less during your meals.** A study in the journal *Obesity (Silver Spring)* found 8 ounces of water before each reduced-calorie meal led to greater fat loss compared to people who didn't drink pre-meal water. Another study presented at the American Chemical Society's annual conference showed 2 glasses of water before every meal helped people lose an average of 15.5 pounds (5 pounds more than the non-water drinkers) over 3 months. Here's the deal: I don't want you drinking too much water *during* meals, when it can dilute your stomach enzymes that break down protein. Before your meal, drink up!

2. **Water can make your skin glow.** I've met women who spend hundreds on to-shelf skincare but ironically don't drink enough water, your first-line defense for healthy, glowing skin. Because skin is your body's largest organ, it's also your largest *detoxification* organ. Perspiration and evaporation continually cleanse your skin and remove waste. Without adequate water, that waste builds up leading to breakouts, acne, and other problems. Poor hydration also means your body can make less new collagen, and the existing collagen becomes brittle.

3. **Water helps muscle maintenance & recovery.** Muscle tissue is about 75% water, which explains why even 3% dehydration can reduce muscle strength up to 15%. Dehydration also shrinks muscle cells and leads to protein breakdown. Optimal hydration replenishes electrolytes and reduces exercise-related inflammation.

4. **If you're not well hydrated, you're not detoxifying.** Even if you're eating organically and following a rigorous cleanse protocol, dehydration means your body can't optimally detoxify. Water flushes waste from your cells, but when you're dehydrated your cells draw water from your blood, stressing your heart and limiting your kidneys from purifying blood.

Your liver and other organs also feel the pressure. Toxic buildup leads to constipation, literally forcing your body to cling to the waste it needs to eliminate.

5. **Dehydration can raise stress hormones.** Some experts believe dehydration is the number-one cause of stress. Even mild dehydration of 1 – 2% can raise levels of your stress hormone cortisol. Among its jobs, cortisol stores fat around your midsection and breaks down muscle.

6. **Dehydration can create fatigue.** Too little water crashes your metabolism to a grinding halt, disrupts fluid balance, and decreases blood volume. Your heart struggles to deliver nutrients and oxygen to various tissues. Headaches, mental fog, and lethargy are among the inevitable results. Ironically, fatigue will probably mean you reach for a java pick-me-up, further dehydrating your body.

7. **Water can reduce cravings.** Thirst can come disguised as hunger, regrettably leading you to those late-afternoon Krispy Kreme donuts your coworker brought in. Before-bed cravings? See if water does the trick: according to a study at the University of Washington, drinking 8 ounces of water at bedtime can shut down your evening hunger pangs.

Coffee When You Cleanse? You Betcha!

I'm going to make a radical claim: a cup of coffee during detoxification is perfectly fine and can even enhance the process. The standard protocol to surrender coffee while detoxifying is an urban legend, and I've seen no evidence to substantiate it.

Before I describe how coffee can benefit detoxification, I want to briefly clarify what I mean by the term. "Don't let the word *detoxification* turn you off," writes Dr. Mark Hyman in The Huffington Post, who says this "is a <u>normal, everyday function</u>. It's the body's way of breaking down and eliminating anything that doesn't belong. And, these days, there are a lot of things our bodies come into contact with that don't belong."

Your liver becomes ground zero for eliminating these toxins. Obviously, while detoxifying, you don't want to add to that burden. Conventional wisdom says coffee can potentially increase your liver's burden, so to play it safe you should eliminate it during detoxification. However, science shows coffee can actually benefit your liver.

One recent study in the journal *Hepatology* involved almost 28,000 people, about half of whom drank coffee. Researchers found those who had three cups a day were <u>about 25 percent less</u>

likely to have abnormal liver enzymes compared with the non-coffee group. Researchers were unsure why, though they credit coffee's thousands of beneficial compounds.

"The results showed that people who said they drank three or more cups of coffee a day had lower levels of all four of these enzymes, compared with people who did not drink any coffee," writes Laura Geggel in The Huffington Post. "Surprisingly, it didn't matter whether a person drank regular or decaf coffee: the effect on liver enzyme levels was almost identical."

Earlier studies also overwhelmingly support coffee's liver-benefitting properties. One 2012 systematic review titled "Impact of Coffee on Liver Diseases", concluded that "coffee appears to have [liver-protecting] health benefits [possibly because of] synergistic effect of multiple compounds…"

What about caffeine? Well, that review mentions that through various mechanisms, caffeine can actually benefit your liver. A study at Duke University found the caffeine equivalent of four cups of coffee or tea a day could prevent or reverse non-alcoholic fatty liver disease (NAFLD). Another found increased caffeine intake could reduce your risk for hepatic fibrosis.

Choosing the Right Coffee Becomes Crucial

You can keep your coffee during detoxification with a few crucial caveats. Coffee type and brewing methods become important here. Studies show filtered coffee provides liver benefits, whereas unfiltered coffee does not. Researchers believe caffeine diter-penes kahweol and cafestol, which are released from ground coffee beans but removed by paper filters, make the difference here.

So stick with filtered, and avoid pesticide-ridden conventional coffee. "Conventional farms apply as much as 250 pounds of chemical fertilizers on every acre," writes Ezra Fieser in The

Christian Science Monitor in an article about why Latin American farmers are abandoning organic coffee.

Mold in coffee can also create a burden to your liver. Mycotoxins, or toxins formed by yeast and fungi, are ubiquitous in conventional coffee, wreaking havoc on your liver and creating a huge impact on how we think and feel.

"Mycotoxins in food and the environment are well documented to increase stress on the liver and kidneys even at levels measured in parts per billion," Dave Asprey, owner of Bulletproof Upgraded Coffee, told me. "Bulletproof beans are lab tested for 27 toxins found in coffee, using proprietary lab tests that detect levels far more accurately than even those used to meet European standards. They meet strict in-house standards designed to support optimal human performance, not just economic goals."

I can attest firsthand to those benefits. Even expensive, organic coffee always left me jittery with a subsequent crash. I didn't feel those affects with Bulletproof because they use the highest-quality beans without the nasty mycotoxins and other problems conventional and even organic coffee frequently present.

Good news: you can keep your coffee while you detoxify, but only if you use Bulletproof Upgraded Coffee.

Coffee Isn't For You? Consider Herbal or Green Teas

Mornings mean coffee for me, and I love having my Bulletproof Upgraded Coffee to start the day focused and full of energy. Not everyone drinks coffee, and don't think you *need* to start drinking coffee for detoxification.

Green and herbal teas are another great way to start your day or provide a mid-afternoon pick-me-up. Green tea especially is good for optimal liver function and helping detoxify. Because most contain less caffeine than coffee (herbal teas are usually caffeine-free), they become a better choice if caffeine leaves you jittery or wired when you should be winding down. Yerba mate, a nutrient-rich drink popular in South America, provides another coffee alternative.

Whatever you choose, opt for organic, high-quality teas, either unsweetened or lightly sweetened with Virgin Diet Sprinkles.

Virgin 7-Day Cleanse Menu

Feel free to drink **Cleansing Green Soup** with your meals or throughout the day if needed.

DAY 1

Breakfast	Coco-Cashew Smoothie
Lunch	Peach-Berry-Almond Smoothie
Dinner	Salmon Puttenesca
	Roasted Acorn Squash Puree
	Serve with a large Detox Salad with Lemon Vinaigrette
Optional Snack	¼ cup Quick Guacamole and crudité

DAY 2

Breakfast	Strawberry Protein "Milkshake"
Lunch	Chocolate and Almond Smoothie
Dinner	Salmon Puttenesca
	Roasted Acorn Squash Puree
	Serve with a large Detox Salad with Apple Cider Vinaigrette
Optional Snack	¼ cup Classic Tapenade on Endive

DAY 3

Breakfast	Chocolate-Cherry-Chia Smoothie
Lunch	Espresso-Almond Smoothie
Dinner	Chicken with 40 Cloves of Garlic
	Wild Rice with Kale and Mushrooms
	Serve with a large Detox Salad with Lemon Vinaigrette
Optional Snack	Kale Chips with Cumin and Sea Salt

DAY 4

Breakfast	Pumpkin Pie Protein Smoothie
Lunch	50/50 Bar Smoothie
Dinner	Chicken with 40 Cloves of Garlic

Wild Rice with Kale and Mushrooms

Serve with a large Detox Salad with Apple Cider Vinaigrette

Optional Snack   2 tablespoon almond butter and celery sticks

DAY 5

Breakfast	Blueberry Ginger Surprise Smoothie
Lunch	Vanilla Pumpkin Spice Latte Smoothie
Dinner	Seared Halibut with Lemon-Basil Gremolata
	Shredded Brussels Sprouts with Easy Lemon Vinaigrette
	Confetti Quinoa
Optional Snack	¼ cup Virgin Diet Hummus Dip and crudité

Day 6

Breakfast	Lean and Green Smoothie
Lunch	Berry Mint Smoothie
Dinner	Seared Halibut with Lemon-Basil Gremolata
	Shredded Brussels Sprouts with Easy Lemon Vinaigrette
	Confetti Quinoa
Optional Snack	Quick Black Bean Dip and crudité

DAY 7

Breakfast	Coconut Lime Smoothie
Lunch	Avo-Raspberry Cream Smoothie
Dinner	Turkey Chili
	Confetti Quinoa
	Serve with a large Detox Salad with Lemon Vinaigrette
Optional Snack	10 – 20 Slow Roasted Nuts

Day 1 Symptoms Checklist
Do you consistently struggle with these symptoms?
Answer Yes or No. A 'maybe' is a Yes.

1.	Energy Levels	❑ YES	❑ NO
2.	Sugar and carb cravings	❑ YES	❑ NO
3.	Sleep quality	❑ YES	❑ NO
4.	Bowel movement regularity	❑ YES	❑ NO
5.	Mood	❑ YES	❑ NO
6.	Productivity	❑ YES	❑ NO
7.	Clarity of thought	❑ YES	❑ NO
8.	Hunger	❑ YES	❑ NO
9.	Motivation	❑ YES	❑ NO
10.	Skin-acne, rashes, rosacea	❑ YES	❑ NO
11.	Gas, bloating, gut issues	❑ YES	❑ NO
12.	Sensitivity to smell	❑ YES	❑ NO
13.	Joint pain	❑ YES	❑ NO
14.	Headaches	❑ YES	❑ NO
15.	Difficulty losing weight	❑ YES	❑ NO

Journal Day 1

Starting:

Weight _____lbs
Body Comp _____% (if available)
Waist Measurement _____inches
Hip Measurement _____inches

Breakfast: Time:_____

_____

_____

Lunch: Time:_____

_____

_____

Dinner: Time:_____

_____

_____

Snack: Time:_____

_____

Water (8-oz): ☐ ☐ ☐ ☐ ☐ ☐ ☐ ☐ ☐ ☐

Lemon-AID: ☐ ☐ ☐ ☐

Other Liquids: _____☐ _____☐ _____☐ _____☐

Notes: _____

Journal Day 2

Breakfast: Time:_____

_____

_____

Lunch: Time:_____

_____

_____

Dinner: Time:_____

_____

_____

Snack: Time:_____

_____

Water (8-oz): ☐ ☐ ☐ ☐ ☐ ☐ ☐ ☐ ☐ ☐

Lemon-AID: ☐ ☐ ☐ ☐

Other Liquids: _____☐ _____☐ _____☐ _____☐

Notes: _____

_____

_____

Journal Day 3

Breakfast: Time:_____

_____

_____

Lunch: Time:_____

_____

_____

Dinner: Time:_____

_____

_____

Snack: Time:_____

_____

Water (8-oz): ☐ ☐ ☐ ☐ ☐ ☐ ☐ ☐ ☐

Lemon-AID: ☐   ☐   ☐   ☐

Other Liquids: _____☐ _____☐ _____☐ _____☐

Notes: _____

_____

_____

Journal Day 4

Breakfast: Time:_____

_____

_____

Lunch: Time:_____

_____

_____

Dinner: Time:_____

_____

_____

Snack: Time:_____

_____

Water (8-oz): ☐ ☐ ☐ ☐ ☐ ☐ ☐ ☐ ☐ ☐

Lemon-AID: ☐ ☐ ☐ ☐

Other Liquids: _____☐ _____☐ _____☐ _____☐

Notes: _____

_____

_____

Journal Day 5

Breakfast: Time:_____

_____

_____

Lunch: Time:_____

_____

_____

Dinner: Time:_____

_____

_____

Snack: Time:_____

_____

Water (8-oz): ☐ ☐ ☐ ☐ ☐ ☐ ☐ ☐ ☐ ☐

Lemon-AID: ☐   ☐   ☐   ☐

Other Liquids: _____☐ _____☐ _____☐ _____☐

Notes: _____

_____

_____

Journal Day 6

Breakfast: Time:_____

_____

_____

Lunch: Time:_____

_____

_____

Dinner: Time:_____

_____

_____

Snack: Time:_____

_____

Water (8-oz): ☐ ☐ ☐ ☐ ☐ ☐ ☐ ☐ ☐ ☐

Lemon-AID: ☐   ☐   ☐   ☐

Other Liquids: _____☐ _____☐ _____☐ _____☐

Notes: _____

_____

_____

Journal Day 7

Breakfast: Time:_____

_____

_____

Lunch: Time:_____

_____

_____

Dinner: Time:_____

_____

_____

Snack: Time:_____

_____

Water (8-oz): ☐ ☐ ☐ ☐ ☐ ☐ ☐ ☐ ☐ ☐

Lemon-AID: ☐   ☐   ☐   ☐

Other Liquids: _____☐ _____☐ _____☐ _____☐

Notes: _____

_____

_____

Day 8 Symptoms Checklist

Do you consistently struggle with these symptoms?
Answer Yes or No. A 'maybe' is a Yes.

1.	Energy Levels	❏ YES	❏ NO
2.	Sugar and carb cravings	❏ YES	❏ NO
3.	Sleep quality	❏ YES	❏ NO
4.	Bowel movement regularity	❏ YES	❏ NO
5.	Mood	❏ YES	❏ NO
6.	Productivity	❏ YES	❏ NO
7.	Clarity of thought	❏ YES	❏ NO
8.	Hunger	❏ YES	❏ NO
9.	Motivation	❏ YES	❏ NO
10.	Skin-acne, rashes, rosacea	❏ YES	❏ NO
11.	Gas, bloating, gut issues	❏ YES	❏ NO
12.	Sensitivity to smell	❏ YES	❏ NO
13.	Joint pain	❏ YES	❏ NO
14.	Headaches	❏ YES	❏ NO
15.	Difficulty losing weight	❏ YES	❏ NO

Day 8 Weight and Measurements:

Weight _____lbs

Body Comp _____% (if available)

Waist Measurement _____inches

Hip Measurement _____inches

Virgin 7-Day Cleanse Shopping List

STAPLES

____ JJ Virgin's All-in-One Chocolate Powder
____ JJ Virgin's All-in-One Vanilla Powder
____ JJ Virgin's Extra Fiber
____ JJ Virgin's Green Balance (optional)
____ JJ Virgin's Virgin Sprinkles (optional)

_____ Flax seed
_____ Chia seeds
_____ Cashew butter
_____ Almond butter
_____ Almond extract
_____ Vanilla extract
_____ Peppermint extract - optional
_____ Cacao nibs
_____ JJ Virgin's All-in-One Bars
_____ Hint Water
_____ Extra virgin olive oil
_____ Palm fruit oil (sustainably farmed)
_____ Coconut oil
_____ Ghee
_____ Macadamia nut oil
_____ Cinnamon
_____ Cumin
_____ Coriander
_____ Chili powder
_____ Basil
_____ Red pepper flakes
_____ Nutmeg
_____ Espresso powder (try Starbucks Via)
_____ Oregano
_____ Paprika
_____ Smoked paprika
_____ Italian seasoning
_____ Pumpkin pie spice
_____ Sea salt
_____ Peppercorns
_____ Tahini
_____ Sherry vinegar
_____ Apple cider vinegar
_____ Pecans
_____ 1-½ cups nuts of choice for Slow Roasted Nuts

_____ Quinoa

_____ Wild rice

_____ Dijon mustard

_____ Capers

_____ Kalamata olives

_____ Picholine olives

_____ Anchovy

_____ Low sodium organic chicken broth

_____ Low sodium organic vegetable broth

_____ 15-oz can garbanzo beans

_____ 15-oz cans black beans

_____ 14.5-oz cans fire-roasted diced tomatoes

_____ 15-oz can no salt added red kidney beans

_____ Tomato paste

_____ 4-oz can diced green chilis

_____ Canned pumpkin

_____ Sunflower seeds

FRESH/FROZEN

_____ So Delicious Dairy Free unsweetened coconut, cashew or almond milk

_____ So Delicious Dairy Free Culinary Coconut Milk

_____ Frozen organic peaches

_____ Frozen organic blueberries

_____ Frozen organic unsweetened strawberries

_____ Frozen organic unsweetened dark cherries

_____ Frozen organic mixed berries

_____ Frozen organic raspberries

_____ Frozen peas

_____ Six-oz salmon fillets

_____ Whole 31/2 – 4 lb chicken

_____ Lean ground turkey

_____ Six-oz halibut fillets

_____ Napa or savoy cabbage

____ Arugula

____ Spinach

____ Radicchio

____ Red onion

____ Mixed veggie for crudité

____ Yellow onions

____ Garlic (lots!!)

____ Container of fresh or jarred chunky salsa

____ Avocados

____ Brussels sprouts

____ Broccoli

____ Celery

____ Shallots

____ Orange

____ Lemon

____ Limes

____ Fresh ginger

____ Yellow bell pepper

____ Red bell pepper

____ Orange bell pepper

____ Mixed mushrooms (shiitake, crimini, chanterelle or oyster)

____ Acorn squash

____ Zucchini

____ Plum tomatoes

____ Cherry/grape tomatoes

____ Fresh basil

____ Fresh parsley

____ Fresh mint leaves

____ Endive

____ Fresh rosemary

____ Fresh thyme

____ Baby spinach

____ Kale

____ Spinach

VIRGIN 7-DAY CLEANSE RECIPES

SNACK RECIPES

Quick Guacamole
But fresh salsa and 4 soft avocados – combine and serve!

Quick Black Bean Dip
Puree one can organic black beans, add 4 ounce can diced green chilis and 1 teaspoon Mexican seasoning

Classic Tapenade on Endive
The Virgin Diet Cookbook
Makes 8 servings

1 cup pitted Kalamata olives
3/4 cup Picholine olives, pitted
1 anchovy
1 garlic clove
2 tablespoons chopped fresh basil
2 tablespoons chopped fresh parsley
2 tablespoons extra virgin olive oil
Fresh endive leaves for serving

Combine the olives, anchovy, garlic, basil, and parsley in the bowl of a food processor. Pulse until the mixture is finely chopped. Transfer to a bowl and stir in the oil.

Spoon a small amount of tapenade onto the end of each endive leaf. Tapenade can me made up to 1 week ahead and kept in the refrigerator in a covered container.

Kale Chips with Cumin and Sea Salt
The Virgin Diet Cookbook
While these may be stored in a covered container for a day or two, kale chips are at their best when eaten the day they are made.

Makes 2-4 servings

1 bunch kale, about 1 pound, washed and thoroughly dried
1 tablespoon olive oil
1/2 teaspoon ground cumin
1/4 teaspoon sea salt
1/8 teaspoon ground chipotle pepper

Preheat the oven to 325°F.

Tear kale into 1 1/2-inch pieces. Toss in a large bowl with the oil, gently rubbing leaves with your fingers to help spread the oil evenly. Add the cumin, salt, and chipotle pepper and toss well.

Arrange kale in a single layer on two large baking sheets. Bake, one batch at a time, turning leaves once, until crisp, 16-18 minutes. Repeat with second batch. Allow kale chips to cool on the pan. Serve immediately or store in a covered container.

Virgin Diet Basic Hummus Dip

Serves 4

2 cups canned garbanzo beans, drained

1/3 cup tahini

1/4 cup lemon juice

1 teaspoon sea salt

2 cloves garlic, crushed

2 tablespoons extra virgin olive oil

1 pinch paprika

Place the garbanzo beans, tahini, lemon juice, olive oil, sea salt and garlic in a blender or food processor. Blend until smooth. Transfer mixture to a serving bowl and sprinkle with paprika. Serve with cucumber, red pepper and jicama spears

Slow Roasted Nuts

Make sure your oven can be set at 140°F, otherwise use a dehydrator.

1 1/2 cups raw nuts (cashews, walnuts, almonds, pecans, macadamia)

1/2 teaspoon sea salt

Place nut in a bowl and add enough water to cover by 3-inches then stir in salt. Let nuts soak overnight.

Preheat the oven to 140°F.

Drain nuts and spread onto a baking sheet or place in a dehydrator. Bake nuts for 8 hours. Remove from the oven or dehydrator and let cool completely (nuts will crisp up as they cool). Store nuts in a resealable plastic bag in the refrigerator for best results.

JJ Virgin's All-in-One bar

16 ounces green drink, <u>greens only juice</u> (no fruit, carrot or beet) or

2 scoops Green Balance and add 2 tablespoons chia or freshly ground flaxseed meal

MEAL RECIPES

.

Cleansing Green Soup

Feel free to have a cup with meals or drink throughout the day if necessary.

Serves 6

1 tablespoon olive oil
1 cup chopped yellow onion
2 teaspoons minced garlic
2 stalks celery, chopped
1 zucchini, chopped

1 cup broccoli florets, chopped

½ cup chopped parsley

½ cup chopped basil

5 cups low sodium vegetable broth

1 cup frozen peas, thawed

3 cups spinach, chopped

3 cups savoy or Napa cabbage, chopped

Sea salt & pepper to taste

- Add olive oil to a large stock pot.
- Add onion and cook, stirring occasionally, until softened, about 5 minutes.
- Add garlic and cook one minute, stirring often.
- Add celery, zucchini, broccoli, parsley and basil and cook 3 minutes, stirring often.
- Add broth and bring to a boil. Reduce heat, cover and simmer 20 minutes.
- Add peas, spinach and cabbage and cook uncovered until greens wilt.
- Transfer to a blender and puree, working in batches.
- Season to taste with salt and pepper.

Detox Salad

4 cups mixed:
Shredded cabbage, arugula, spinach, chopped radicchio Red onion, finely sliced

Toss and serve with one of the two vinaigrettes below.

Lemon
Vinaigrette

Makes approximately 1/3 cup

2 tablespoons lemon juice
1 teaspoon minced shallot
½ teaspoon lemon zest
½ teaspoon fresh thyme leaves, chopped
¼ cup extra virgin olive oil
Pinch sea salt & pepper

Place lemon juice, shallot, zest and thyme leaves in a small bowl. Blend well.

Slowly whisk in the oil in a steady stream.

Season to taste with salt and pepper.

Apple Cider Vinaigrette

Makes approximately 1/3 cup

2 tablespoons apple cider vinegar
1 teaspoon minced garlic
1 teaspoon minced fresh chives
¼ cup extra virgin olive oil
½ teaspoon Dijon mustard
Pinch sea salt & pepper

Place vinegar, garlic, chives and mustard in a small bowl. Blend well.

Slowly whisk in the oil in a steady stream.

Season to taste with salt and pepper.

Salmon Puttenesca

The Virgin Diet Cookbook
Serves 4

4 teaspoons olive oil, divided
1 small onion, chopped
2 garlic cloves, minced
1/2 teaspoon dried basil
1/8 teaspoon crushed red pepper flakes
1/3 cup pitted Calamata olives, halved lengthwise
2 teaspoons drained capers, chopped
1 pint grape tomatoes, halved lengthwise
2 tablespoons chopped fresh parsley
1/2 teaspoon sea salt, divided
4 (6-ounce) wild salmon filets, such as king or sockeye
1/8 teaspoon freshly ground black pepper

Heat 2 teaspoons of the oil in a large nonstick skillet over medium-high heat. Add the onion, garlic, basil, and pepper flakes and cook, stirring, 1 minute. Add the olives and capers and cook 1 minute. Add the tomatoes and cook, stirring occasionally, until wilted, 3-4 minutes. Transfer to a bowl and stir in the parsley and 1/4 teaspoon of the salt.

Season the salmon with remaining 1/4 teaspoon salt and pepper. Wipe out the skillet; add the remaining 2 teaspoons oil and heat over medium. Add salmon to the skillet flesh side down; cook 4-5 minutes per side, until the fish flakes easily with a fork. Serve topped with tomato mixture.

Roasted Acorn Squash Puree

The Virgin Diet Cookbook
Other squash, including butternut and kabocha, may be substituted
Serves 4

1 acorn squash, about 2 1/4 pounds, cut in half and seeds removed
1 tablespoon macadamia nut oil
pinch ground nutmeg
1/2 teaspoon sea salt
1/8 teaspoon freshly ground black pepper

Preheat the oven to 400°F. Lightly oil and 11 x 7-inch baking dish

Place squash cut side down in the prepared baking dish. Cover with aluminum foil and roast until very tender, about 55-60 minutes. Remove from the oven and cool 10 minutes.

When cool enough to handle, use a spoon to scoop out flesh and transfer to a food processor. Puree the squash; transfer to a medium nonstick skillet over medium-high heat and cook, stirring, until squash mixture is somewhat drier, about 4 minutes. Remove from the heat and stir in the oil, salt, and pepper.

Chicken with 40 Cloves of Garlic

The Virgin Diet Cookbook
Serves 6

2 tablespoons olive oil
2 tablespoons chopped fresh rosemary
3/4 teaspoon sea salt
1/2 teaspoon freshly ground black pepper
3 1/2-4 pound whole chicken
40 garlic cloves, unpeeled
1 onion, chopped
2 celery ribs, chopped
1 1/2 cups low sodium organic chicken broth

Preheat the oven to 400°F.

Stir the oil, rosemary, salt, and pepper together to form a paste. Use your fingertips to gently loosen the skin over the breast meat, legs, and thighs. Rub the paste under the skin and over the meat. Tuck the wings under the bird and tie the legs with kitchen twine. Transfer the chicken to a shallow roasting pan and add the garlic, onion, celery, and broth.

Roast the chicken until a thermometer inserted into the thickest part of the thigh registers 170°F, about 65-70 minutes. Remove from the oven and let chicken cool 5 minutes. Remove the skin, carve chicken and serve with garlic cloves and pan juices.

Wild Rice with Kale and Mushrooms

The Sugar Impact Diet Collaborative Cookbook by Steven Masley
This is a flavorful side dish. As a double portion, it makes a light meal. "Wild rice" isn't actually rice but a grass, which cooks like rice and is loaded with delicious nutrients. And the kale makes it very colorful and healthful! Dr. Masley's recipe was adapted from *The 30-Day Heart Tune Up*.
Serves 4

1 cup wild rice
4 cups water
1 cup low-sodium chicken or vegetable stock
1 tablespoon virgin olive oil
1 medium onion, diced
¼ teaspoon sea salt
¼ teaspoon ground black pepper
1 teaspoon Italian herbs
4 cups wild mushrooms (shiitake, crimini, chantrelle, or oyster)
4 cups kale, tough stems removed, chopped into thin slices
15 ounces garbanzo beans, cooked, rinsed, and drained
2 tablespoons pecans, chopped

Combine wild rice, water, and stock in a pot, bring to a boil. Simmer for 50 minutes until rice is barely firm. Drain and set aside.

10 minutes before rice is ready, heat a large sauté pan to medium-high and add oil, onion, salt, pepper, and herbs.

Sauté one minute, with occasional stirring. Add mushrooms and sauté an additional 2 minutes until mushrooms soften. Add kale and garbanzo beans, reduce heat to medium, cover, heat 2 minutes, and remove from heat. When rice is cooked and drained, mix with sautéed vegetables. Serve garnished with pecans.

Seared Halibut with Lemon-Basil Gremolata

Sugar Impact Diet Cookbook – May 2015

If you're not familiar with the Italian condiment gremolata, you'll be surprised at how much its few, simple ingredients sass up this halibut. Gremolata is traditionally made with parsley, lemon, and raw garlic, but I've refined it by using fresh basil and cooking the garlic to take the edge off.

Makes 4 servings

4 (6-ounce) skinless halibut fillets
1 tablespoon Dijon mustard
1/2 teaspoon sea salt
1/4 teaspoon ground black pepper
2 tablespoons olive oil
3 garlic cloves, minced
1 large plum tomato, seeded and chopped
3 tablespoons chopped basil
1 tablespoon grated lemon zest

Brush the halibut fillets with the mustard and season with salt and pepper.

Heat 1 tablespoon of the oil in a large nonstick skillet over medium-high. Add the halibut, flesh side down, and cook 5 minutes. Turn the halibut over and cook until the fish flakes easily with a fork, about 5 minutes longer. Transfer to a plate.

Heat the remaining 1 tablespoon oil and stir in the garlic; cook, stirring, until fragrant, 30 seconds. Add the tomato and cook until starting to wilt, 1-2 minutes. Remove from the heat and stir in the basil and lemon zest. Spoon the tomato mixture over halibut to serve.

Shredded Brussels Sprouts with Lemon Vinaigrette

The Sugar Impact Diet Cookbook – May 2015
Makes 4 servings

1 tablespoon olive oil
1 medium red onion, thinly sliced
4 garlic cloves, sliced
1 1/2 pounds Brussels sprouts, very thinly sliced
2 tablespoons Slow Roasted Almonds (recipe above in Snacks), chopped
3 tablespoons Lemon Vinaigrette
1/4 teaspoon sea salt
1/8 teaspoon freshly ground black pepper

Heat the oil in a large nonstick skillet over medium-high. Add the onion and garlic and cook, stirring occasionally, until slightly softened, 2-3 minutes. Add the Brussels sprouts and cook, stirring occasionally, until crisp-tender and lightly browned, 7-8 minutes. Add the almonds and cook 1 minute longer. Remove from the heat and stir in the vinaigrette, salt and pepper.

Confetti Quinoa

The Virgin Diet Cookbook
Makes 4 servings

1 cup dry quinoa
3/4 teaspoon sea salt, divided
4 teaspoons coconut oil
1 large shallot, finely chopped
3 garlic cloves, minced
2 teaspoons chopped fresh thyme
1 medium red bell pepper, finely chopped
1 medium orange bell pepper, finely chopped
1 medium yellow bell pepper, finely chopped
1 teaspoon ground coriander
1/4 cup sunflower seeds
1 tablespoon sherry vinegar
1/4 teaspoon freshly ground black pepper

Cook quinoa with 1/4 teaspoon of the salt according to package directions.

Heat the oil in a large nonstick skillet over medium-high. Add the shallot, garlic and thyme and cook 1 minute. Stir in the bell peppers and coriander and cook until crisp tender, 3-4 minutes.

Add the sunflower seeds and cook 1 minute. Stir in the quinoa and cook, stirring, 1 minute until well mixed and heated through. Remove from the heat and stir in the vinegar, remaining ½ teaspoon salt and pepper.

Turkey Chili

The Virgin Diet Cookbook
Makes 4 servings

1 tablespoon palm fruit oil
1 medium onion, chopped
4 garlic cloves, minced
1 large green bell pepper, chopped
1 pound lean ground turkey
5 teaspoons chili powder
1 teaspoon smoked paprika
1/2 teaspoon dried oregano
2 (14.5-ounce) cans fire roasted diced tomatoes
2 tablespoons tomato paste
1 (15-ounce) can organic no salt added red kidney beans, drained and rinsed
1/2 teaspoon sea salt
1/4 teaspoon freshly ground black pepper

Heat the oil in a large saucepan or Dutch oven over medium-high heat. Add the onion, garlic and bell pepper and cook, stirring occasionally, until the vegetables begin to soften, 2-3 minutes. Add the turkey and cook, breaking it into smaller pieces, until no longer pink, about 5-6 minutes. Stir in the chili powder, paprika and oregano and cook 1 minute. Add the tomatoes and tomato paste, bring to a boil and immediately reduce the heat to medium-low; cover and simmer, stirring occasionally, 30 minutes or until slightly thickened.

Stir in the beans and cook 5 minutes longer. Remove from the heat and stir in the salt and pepper.

Virgin 7-Day Cleanse - Vegan Menu

Feel free to drink **Cleansing Green Soup** (substitute ghee with olive oil) with your meals or throughout the day if needed.

DAY 1
Breakfast	Coco-Cashew Smoothie
Lunch	Peach-Berry-Almond Smoothie
Dinner	Black Bean and Butternut Squash Chili
	Serve with a large Detox Salad with Lemon Vinaigrette
Optional Snack	¼ cup Guacamole and crudité

DAY 2
Breakfast	Strawberry Protein "Milkshake"
Lunch	Chocolate and Almond Smoothie
Dinner	Black Bean and Butternut Squash Chili
	Serve with a large Detox Salad with Apple Cider Vinaigrette
Optional Snack	10-20 Slow Roasted Nuts

DAY 3
Breakfast	Chocolate-Cherry-Chia Smoothie
Lunch	Espresso-Almond Smoothie
Dinner	Chickpea & Veggie Sliders
	Serve with a large Detox Salad with Lemon Vinaigrette

| Optional Snack | Kale Chips with Cumin and Sea Salt |

DAY 4
Breakfast	Pumpkin Pie Protein Smoothie
Lunch	50/50 Bar
Dinner	Chickpea and Veggie Sliders
	Serve with a large Detox Salad with Apple Cider Vinaigrette
Optional Snack	2 tablespoons almond butter and celery sticks

DAY 5
Breakfast	Blueberry Ginger Surprise Smoothie
Lunch	Vanilla Pumpkin Spice Latte Smoothie
Dinner	Lentil Nut Burgers with Cilantro Vinaigrette
	Serve with a large Detox Salad with Lemon Vinaigrette
Optional Snack	¼ cup Virgin Diet Hummus Dip and crudité

DAY 6
Breakfast	Lean and Green Smoothie
Lunch	Berry Mint Smoothie
Dinner	Lentil Nut Burgers with Cilantro Vinaigrette
	Serve with a large Detox Salad with Apple Cider Vinaigrette
Optional Snack	Quick Black Bean Dip and crudité

DAY 7
Breakfast	Coconut Lime Smoothie
Lunch	Avo-Raspberry Cream Smoothie
Dinner	Wild Rice with Kale and Mushrooms
	Serve with a large Detox Salad with Lemon Vinaigrette
Optional Snack	10 – 20 Slow Roasted Nuts

Virgin 7-Day Cleanse Vegan Shopping List

STAPLES FOR VEGAN 7 DAY CLEANSE

_____ JJ Virgin's Plant-Based All-in-One Chocolate Powder
_____ JJ Virgin's Plant-Based All-in-One Vanilla Powder
_____ JJ Virgin's Extra Fiber
_____ JJ Virgin's Green balance (optional)
_____ JJ Virgin's Virgin Sprinkles (optional)
_____ Flax seed

_____ Chia seeds

_____ Cashew butter

_____ Almond butter

_____ Almond extract

_____ Vanilla extract

_____ Peppermint extract - optional

_____ Cacao nibs

_____ JJ Virgin All-in-One Bars

_____ Hint Water

_____ Extra virgin olive oil

_____ Apple cider vinegar

_____ Coconut oil

_____ Cinnamon

_____ Cumin

_____ Coriander

_____ Chili powder

_____ Cayenne pepper - optional

_____ Espresso powder (try Starbucks Via)

_____ Paprika

_____ Mexican Seasoning

_____ Pumpkin pie spice

_____ Sea salt

_____ Peppercorns

_____ Tahini

_____ Walnuts

_____ 1-½ cups nuts of choice for Slow Roasted Nuts

_____ Quinoa

_____ Brown rice

_____ Low sodium organic vegetable broth

_____ 15-oz can garbanzo beans

_____ 15-oz cans black beans

_____ 15 oz can chickpeas

_____ 15-oz can organic black lentils

_____ 4-oz can diced green chilis

_____ Canned pumpkin

FRESH/FROZEN

____ So Delicious Dairy Free unsweetened coconut, cashew or almond milk

____ So Delicious Dairy Free Culinary Coconut Milk

____ Frozen organic peaches

____ Frozen organic blueberries

____ Frozen organic unsweetened strawberries

____ Frozen organic unsweetened dark cherries

____ Frozen organic mixed berries

____ Frozen organic raspberries

____ Frozen peas

____ Savoy or Napa cabbage

____ Arugula

____ Spinach

____ Radicchio

____ Red onion

____ Mixed veggie for crudité

____ Yellow onions

____ Garlic

____ Container of fresh or jarred chunky salsa

____ Avocados

____ Scallions (green onions)

____ Celery

____ Carrots

____ Shallots

____ Cilantro

____ Jalapeño peppers

____ Broccoli

____ Orange

____ Lemon

____ Limes

____ Fresh ginger

____ White mushrooms

____ Butternut squash

____ Zucchini

____ Tomatoes

____ Fresh parsley

____ Fresh basil

____ Fresh mint leaves

____ Baby kale

____ Baby spinach

____ Kale

____ Spinach

VIRGIN 7-DAY CLEANSE
VEGAN RECIPES

Black Bean and Butternut Squash Chili

The Sugar Impact Diet 2-Week Cookbook
Serves 4

2 tablespoons extra virgin olive oil
1 medium yellow onion, chopped
1 celery stalk, chopped
1 medium carrot, diced

1 tablespoon chopped shallot
1 jalapeno pepper, seeded and chopped
2 teaspoons chopped garlic
2 cups peeled, diced butternut squash
2 ½ cup vegetable broth
3 15-oz cans black beans, drained and rinsed
2 cups chopped tomato
2 tablespoons chili powder
1 teaspoon cumin
1 teaspoon coriander
1 tablespoon lime juice
Salt & pepper to taste
Pinch cayenne, optional

Heat oil in a large saucepan over medium heat. Add onion, celery, carrot and shallot and sauté 4-5 minutes until softened.

Add jalapeno pepper and garlic and cook 2 minutes, stirring occasionally. Add butternut and sauté for 2 minutes, stirring occasionally.

Stir in the veg broth, beans, tomatoes, chili powder, cumin and coriander. Bring to a boil, reduce heat, cover and simmer 15-20 minutes, until butternut is tender.

Stir in lime juice and season to taste with salt, pepper and cayenne, if using.

Chickpea & Veggie Sliders

The Sugar Impact Diet 2-Week Cookbook
Serves 4

½ cup quinoa
1 15-oz can chickpeas beans, rinsed and drained
2 carrots, grated
1 jalapeno pepper, seeded and minced
1 scallion, minced
2 teaspoons lemon zest
1 teaspoon lemon juice
1 tablespoon ground flax meal
3 tablespoons water
Sea salt & pepper to taste
1-2 tablespoon coconut oil
4 cups baby kale
Juice of 1 lemon
1 avocado, chopped

Bring 1 cup of water to boil in small saucepan. Add quinoa, reduce heat, cover and simmer 13 minutes. Remove from heat and let stand 5 minutes. Drain any excess liquid and turn onto baking sheet to cool.

In a food processor, pulse beans until coarsely chopped. Place in a bowl with the cooled quinoa. Add carrot, jalapeno, scallion, zest and juice, mixing well.

In a small bowl, whisk ground flax meal with water let sit 2 minutes. Add flax slurry to bean mixture and stir to combine. Season to taste with salt and pepper.

Heat oil in skillet over medium high heat. Add ¼ cup of mixture to skillet and flatten with spatula. Repeat with remaining mixture, cooking in batches, and adding more oil, if necessary. (Don't overcrowd your skillet with sliders or they will steam and not brown.)

Cook 3-4 minutes per side until browned and cooked through.

Meanwhile toss baby kale with lemon juice and divide among 4 plates. Place sliders on top of greens and top with chopped avocado.

Lentil Nut Burgers with Cilantro Vinaigrette

The Virgin Diet Cookbook
Makes 4 servings

2 tablespoons chopped fresh cilantro
1 tablespoon fresh lime juice
1/2 teaspoon grated fresh lime zest
1/2 teaspoon salt, divided
4 tablespoons olive oil, divided
1 cup chopped white mushrooms, about 4 ounces
1 small onion, finely chopped, about 1/4 cup
3 cloves garlic minced
1 teaspoon ground cumin
1/3 cup walnuts, finely chopped
1 (15-ounce) can organic black lentils, drained and rinsed
1 cup cooked brown rice
2 tablespoons chopped fresh parsley
1/4 teaspoon freshly ground black pepper

Sliced cucumbers (optional)
Sliced tomatoes (optional)
Sliced fennel (optional)

Make the dressing: combine the cilantro, lime juice, zest, and ¼ teaspoon of the salt in a small bowl; lowly whisk in 2 tablespoons of the oil in a steady stream. Set aside.

Heat 2 teaspoons of the oil in a medium nonstick skillet over medium heat. Add the mushrooms, onion, garlic, and cumin and cook until softened, 4-5 minutes. Add the walnuts and cook until nuts are lightly toasted, 2-3 minutes. Transfer mixture to a bowl.

Combine the lentils and rice in the bowl of a food processor and pulse until the mixture is coarsely chopped; add to mushroom mixture. Stir in the parsley, remaining ¼ teaspoon salt and pepper. Form into four 1/2-inch thick patties.

Heat the remaining 4 teaspoons oil in a large nonstick skillet over medium heat. Add the patties and cook, turning once, until browned and heated through, 9-10 minutes. Transfer to serving plates and top with vinaigrette.

Bonus points to support detoxification

Sauna

For enhanced fat loss, detoxification and optimal health, consider a full spectrum infrared sauna.

I've long been a fan of infrared saunas. Recently I took that love to the next level and splurged on one for my home. I didn't make that decision lightly. After careful research and speaking with trusted colleagues, I opted for a <u>Sunlighten sauna</u>, the only brand clinically shown to raise core temperature so you burn more fat and more effectively detoxify.

I'm a science person, and I want research to substantiate my decisions. Well, Sunlighten delivered it. Based on 56 clinical studies, their unique patented technology provides near, mid, and far infrared at optimal wavelengths.

"I just can't handle the heat," someone will occasionally say when I tell them about saunas.

If you've ever experienced a traditional sauna, you know it can quickly become uncomfortably hot. Not infrared heat, which feels like lying in the sun on a warm day and letting heat penetrate your skin. That's because whereas traditional saunas operate in excess of 200°F, infrared heat can provide those same benefits at a far more comfortable 100° - 130°F temperature.

A quick PubMed search reveals infrared saunas have an impressive amount of supporting research. One review in the journal *Canadian Family Physician* showed among its many benefits, far-infrared saunas could help normalize blood pressure, relieve chronic pain, help heal chronic fatigue syndrome, and even promote weight loss.

Another study in the journal *Alternative Therapies in Health and Medicine* found saunas could help remove heavy metals and chemical xenobiotics. Researchers concluded that "saunas are safe and effective and should be used more frequently to benefit [your] health."

Let's look briefly at two significant benefits.

Detoxification

We tend to think of detoxifying as something to do twice a year, yet your cells constantly detoxify. Providing them the correct nourishment along with other measures to optimally do their job becomes essential, whether you're doing a deep-dive detox or just want to reduce your toxic load. That's where an infrared sauna comes in.

Researchers have long told us how the body sweats out toxic substances, including heavy metals. As long as you maintain proper hydration, the more you safely sweat, the more toxins you'll expel from your body. A far infrared sauna provides the safest, most effective way to literally sweat out those toxins to reduce symptoms, boost immunity, and increase overall health and vitality.

Sunlighten saunas are seven times more effective to help your body detoxify than a traditional sauna, thanks to their highly efficient, patented infrared heating technology, which is the only technology proven to raise core body temperature two to three degrees.

By raising the body's core temperature, infrared saunas can produce a sweat composed of 20% toxins versus only 3% toxins with a traditional sauna. You get a deep, detoxifying sweat that penetrates and releases toxins at the cellular level.

Fast, Lasting Fat Loss

Infrared saunas can also help burn fat. In a 2009 study, Sunlighten infrared saunas helped lower weight and waist circumference in just three months. Participants in that study felt far infrared sauna use was similar to moderate exercise but "much more relaxing."

Another study published in the *Journal of the American Medical Association* found infrared saunas could help you burn up to 600 calories in just 40 minutes. That's because during a sauna weight loss session, core temperatures increase, forcing your body to cool itself and creating a healthy sweat. Using an infrared sauna increases heart rate, cardiac output, metabolic rate, and blood flow, burning more calories and creating more fat loss.

Not all infrared saunas are the same. Low-end saunas are most likely only generating a small amount of infrared. I bought a Sunlighten sauna because it is proven 99% effective.

What impresses me most about Sunlighten are the preset wellness programs. With one touch, I can select detoxification, cardio, relaxation, pain relief, weight loss, or anti-aging. The heaters will emit the optimal blend of near, mid and far infrared wavelengths based on clinical data. I love the customization feature!

Now, you know I'm big on eating clean and exercising. I don't want you to think you can eat high-sugar impact foods, blow off your workout, and then hit the sauna to magically sweat away those excess calories.

That said, when you want every tool in your health arsenal to burn fat, effectively detoxify, and maintain optimal health, a sauna can provide just the boost you need while providing a wonderful way to relax and release stress.

Dry brushing

With all the focus on your liver, you might not consider your skin as a detoxification. Yet every day, your skin releases waste through your pores. In fact, every minute we lose about 30,000 dead skin cells, which constantly become replaced.

Dry brushing can help here. Regularly dry brushing increases circulation and improves lymphatic flow, pulling away toxin-loaded dead cells and stimulating growth of healthy new cells.

If you're new to dry brushing, look for a natural bristle brush at your local health food store. Start with light, gentle brushing and eventually your skin will handle more invigorating brushing. Stroke the brush toward the heart. When you dry brush your stomach, go in a clockwise motion, which works with the natural digestive flow.

You want dry, but not incredibly dry, skin when you dry brush. (If your skin is incredibly dry, try coconut oil while you brush, but clean your brush sufficiently afterwards.) Avoid brushing over cuts and other wounds. Immediately shower after you dry brush to remove those dead skin cells.

Source: http://www.naturalnews.com/040615_dry_brushing_lymphatic_system_detox.html#ixzz3Li9gtY8L

Massage

Do you really need an excuse for a massage? Well, you've got science on your side: One study found massage therapy reduces your stress hormone cortisol while boosting feel-good serotonin and dopamine. That's especially good news while you're detoxifying and want to let go of stress, anxiety, and other negative feelings.

Massages improve circulation and optimize lympathic function so you flush out toxins while boosting immunity. A massage also creates "me" time, which you'll want to create more of while you detoxify to relax and rejuvenate.

Epsom salts bath

A warm bath with Epsom salt, which provides a valuable source of magnesium, can help you relax as you detoxify. Add two cups of Epsom salts three times week to your bath. If bathing isn't for you, consider rubbing Epsom salts with a warm, wet washcloth in the bath or shower.

Designs for Health Detox Packets

All the vitamins, minerals, antioxidants, and other nutrients your liver requires for phase 1 and 2 detoxification in optimal, highly absorbable amounts, in one easy-to-take packet. No sorting, counting, or measuring. Just take one packet with a meal or smoothie and you're providing your liver all the essential nutrients for optimal detoxification.

JJ Virgin's Microbiome Balance

Optimal detoxification begins with a healthy gut. Microbiome Balance is a dairy-free bacteriophage/probiotic combination formula that supports the proliferation of beneficial bacteria throughout the small and large intestines to promote healthy gut and immune function. Just one delayed-release capsule increases intact delivery to the small intestine by protecting these organisms from stomach acid. Microbiome Balance does not cause gas or bloating like some probiotics.

JJ Virgin's Digestive Enzymes

If you're not breaking down your food, you're not fully detoxifying. That's where my Digestive Enzymes can help. This unique formula slows or even blocks carbohydrate digestion while optimizing fat and protein digestion. These Digestive Enzymes can help support the body during times of stress when our own digestive enzymes can be less available and effective as well as through the natural decline in enzyme availability and activity that starts around age 35.

Yoga

Many people designate detoxifying as a more centering, introspective time. That might mean you avoid lifting heavy or burst training while you're detoxifying. (Although keep in mind, you *can* still do stimulating, challenging exercise while you detoxify.)

Yoga provides a gentler alternative that combines exercise with stretching, meditation, and tuning in to your body's natural rhythm. Yoga improves circulation and stimulates blood flow, enhancing the detoxifying process. You'll probably also find a yoga practice simultaneously relaxing and rejuvenating.

Yoga practices are all over the map. Some focus on gentle stretching and restorative poses. Others become vigorous and intense. If you're a yoga newbie, shop around and find a class, instructor, or DVD that works for your goals and personality.

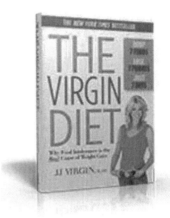

Overview of the Virgin Diet

The Virgin Diet is a 3-cycle plan that involves removing seven highly reactive (high-FI) foods. High-FI stands for High "food intolerance". Let's briefly look at each cycle.

Cycle 1

This cycle produces dramatic and fast fat loss. A study from the *International Journal of Behavioral Medicine* showed that people who lose weight fast are five times more likely to keep it off for 18 months than people who lose weight more slowly.

You will *completely* eliminate all seven top-FI foods in Cycle 1. The seven high-FI foods are:

- Gluten
- Soy
- Dairy
- Eggs
- Peanuts
- Corn
- Sugar and artificial sweeteners

You cannot do just a "little" of these foods. You must completely remove them for three weeks to recover from the inflammation and get rid of the immune complexes that create uncomfortable symptoms such as joint pain, headaches, bloating, gas, fatigue, and brain fog.

Even a little of the high-FI foods during this period will trigger the release of these IgG antibodies and create more immune complexes, unraveling your healing process.

You must always read labels, since many processed and packaged foods contain hidden sources of these high-FI foods.

To avoid deprivation, you're going to create *lateral shifts* to replace these seven high-FI foods. The right foods will help heal your body, maintain steady blood sugar, reduce inflammation, improve digestion, and trigger fast fat loss.

So what *do* you eat when you eliminate these seven high-FI foods? Plenty:

- You start your morning with JJ Virgin's All-in-One Shake (or an acceptable shake following the aforementioned guidelines) with berries, flax or chia seeds in So Delicious unsweetened coconut milk. It's fast, filling, inexpensive, and keeps you full for hours.

The Virgin Diet Basic Shake Recipe
2 scoops JJ Virgin's All-In-One Shake
1 serving JJ Virgin's Extra Fiber
1 serving frozen fruit (we recommend organic berries)
Handful of fresh or frozen spinach or kale
8-10 ounces So Delicious Dairy Free unsweetened coconut milk

Add-ins:
1 tablespoon of nut butter
1 tablespoon chia, hemp, or freshly ground flaxseed meal
1 scoop JJ Virgin's Green Balance

- Every meal consists of:
  - Clean lean protein – top choices include wild-caught fish; grass-fed beef; free-range chicken and other poultry; pastured pork, lamb, pea & plant based protein powders
  - Plenty of green leafy veggies
  - High-fiber starchy carbs – sweet potatoes, lentils and other legumes, and quinoa
  - Good fats – avocado, nuts and seeds, coconut oil/milk, olive oil

The good news is that people lose up to seven pounds during the first week on Cycle 1 when they eliminate these seven high-FI foods. But you can't do it halfway: you have to completely remove them for three weeks to get these benefits.

Cycle 2

Cycle 2 helps you customize your diet and discover which high-FI foods are really causing you trouble. In this cycle, you will re-introduce one high-FI food – gluten, soy, dairy and eggs – every week to see if you can incorporate that food back into your diet.

(The other high-FI foods – corn, peanuts, sugar and artificial sweeteners – should either take a permanent vacation from your diet or be eaten very sparingly.)

You might have considered these foods healthy and eaten them every day for years without connecting them to your symptoms. When you re-introduce each of these four foods, you will soon know whether you have a reaction and whether or not you can re-incorporate that food into your diet.

Cycle 3

In this cycle you learn long-term maintenance strategies to keep your weight off and stay lean and sexy for life. Many programs focus only on fat loss but not maintenance.

Cycle 3 is about utilizing the right exercise, lifestyle measures, and other components to stay lean and healthy for life. You'll receive effective strategies that help you make fat loss permanent and easy. You'll also learn why it's important to do Cycle 1 and completely eliminate the seven high-FI foods once a year.

To learn more about The Virgin Diet, please visit www. thevirgindiet.com.

Overview of Sugar Impact Diet

I designed The Sugar Impact Diet to help you gradually shift from a high-sugar impact (SI) diet to a low-SI diet. It's essential that you transition your diet gradually to avoid withdrawal and cravings that can set you back, which is why there are three cycles in the program. Let's briefly look at how each cycle works.

Cycle 1— Taper

The first step is to identify what's sabotaging your weight and health. Where are the sugar landmines in your diet? You'll figure that out by taking the **Sneaky Sugar Inventory.** Then you'll take the **Sugar Impact Quiz** to see how these sneaky sugars are impacting your overall health.

Once you pinpoint the sneaky sugars that are sabotaging your health, Cycle 1 will help you step away from them slowly, easing you from high-SI foods to medium-SI foods.

Remember, you're not going cold turkey in Cycle 1! You're going to trade and taper with swaps. Nothing is cut from your diet without being replaced. Depending on where you start on the **Sugar Impact Quiz**, you'll spend 1 or 2 weeks in Cycle 1.

This time is necessary to lay the groundwork for Cycle 2. As you swap high-SI foods for medium-SI foods, you'll begin your shift from sugar burner to fat burner— and seeing the change in your energy levels and on the scale will be the motivation you need to stay on the plan until you're ready to move to Cycle 2.

Cycle 2— Transition

In Cycle 2, you'll really see the weight fall off and you'll truly reset your body and taste buds after years of eating the wrong way. During Cycle 2 you'll swap medium-SI foods for low-SI foods, and your metabolism will shift from burning sugar to burning fat!

Let's talk a little bit about fat loss. The average person loses 10 pounds during these 2 weeks! As the weight melts off, you're letting your taste buds come back to life and you're retraining them to appreciate what natural sweetness really means.

Cycle 3— Transformed!

By the time you get to Cycle 3, you'll feel like a new person: lighter, more energetic, and more in tune with how your body is designed to eat. Many clients feel so great by the time they get to Cycle 3 that they don't want to reintroduce any high-SI foods! But the last thing I want is for you to gradually slip back into your old high-SI habits over time.

That's where Cycle 3 comes in. This cycle is all about customizing the program to your body and your long-term goals. Using the **Sugar Impact Quiz**, you'll determine how much sugar you can handle on a daily basis without unraveling all your progress and without losing the great feeling that comes with low-SI living. Your quiz results will help you create a maintenance program that works specifically for you and builds on your success going forward.

RESOURCES

JJ VIRGIN's ALL-IN-ONE PROTEIN POWDERS
www.virginstore.com

Plant-Based
For those who prefer plant-based proteins, the newly reformulated Virgin Diet Plant-Based All-In-One Shakes offer a combination of low allergenicity proteins including pea, chia and chlorella with only 1 gram of sugar, no xanthan gum, and improved flavor.

   All of our protein products are free of gluten, dairy, egg, soy and artificial sweeteners.

   JJ Virgin's Plant Based All-in-One Chocolate
   JJ Virgin's Plant Based All-in-One Vanilla
   JJ Virgin's Plant Based All-in-One Chai

Paleo-Inspired

For our Paleo dieters, and those bodies that respond better to animal protein, we offer the JJ Virgin's All-In-One Shakes that give you the power of beef protein without all that fat and cholesterol and with amazing bio-availability.

All of our protein products are free of gluten, dairy, egg, soy and artificial sweeteners.

JJ Virgin's All-in-One Chocolate
JJ Virgin's All-in-One Vanilla

JJ Virgin's Extra Fiber

Extra Fiber can be a powerful tool to support proper weight management, glucose levels and lipid levels, but remember to start slow and increase a little at a time. This will not only yield the best results, but will give you all the benefits of fiber without the gas and bloating that can come with a rapid change in your intake of healthy fiber. Because **JJ Virgin's** Extra Fiber is tasteless, odorless, and dissolves readily in water, it can be easily mixed with a morning smoothie or any preferred beverage.

JJ Virgin's Extra Fiber is a grain free, Paleo-safe fiber option to support you, not only in weight loss, but also in supporting healthy bowel movements and a happier microbiome (your gut environment).

JJ Virgin's Green Balance

Consuming the 10 servings of vegetables I recommend can be a challenge for many of us. That is why I created Green Balance, which gives you the alkalizing, phytonutrient-rich power of additional greens plus the beneficial powers of fruits without their sugars and a healthy dose of fiber. Green Balance includes a mixed blend of 12 different kinds of soluble and insoluble fiber that slows the absorption to prevent the blood sugar spikes that can happen with common green drinks.

- Easy-to-absorb powdered greens with the stabilizing effects of fiber to slow absorption.
- Simulates that experience of greens consumption.
- Detoxification and alkalizing power of greens without the sugar spike that fiber-less greens can cause.
- Made from vegetables with high ORAC values (a rating system for the amount and quality of antioxidants in foods).
- Phytonutrient-rich greens with 12 different types of soluble and insoluble fiber.

Delicious cranberry-orange flavor, made lightly sweet with a prebiotic fiber called inulin.

JJ Virgin's Virgin Sprinkles

Delicious taste with health benefits! A blend of all natural, beneficial sweeteners that tastes like sugar and mixes easily into your favorite foods or beverages.

A proprietary blend of glycine, erythritol and stevia that don't cause the stomach upset or bloating often associated with sugar alcohols.

- Glycine has the power to regulate blood sugar by converting glucose into energy, making it an ideal sweetener to stabilize blood sugar levels for people with insulin resistance and diabetes.
- Erythritol is rapidly absorbed in the small intestine and very little make it through to your colon, reducing the

gas, bloating and other side effects that are common with other sugar alcohols.

- Stevia has been shown to modestly improve insulin action and improve metabolic syndrome in rats.

JJ Virgin's Bars

When you want a healthy, delicious snack or mini-meal, the convenient JJ Virgin's Bars give you a protein and slow, low carb energy boost with minimal sugar. They are available in three tasty flavors that make use of fresh organic ingredients like cashew butter, walnuts, chia seeds, cacao nibs and more. You'll love the convenience and taste of these bars that are appropriate for all three Cycles of The Virgin Diet and Sugar Impact Diet

- Cinnamon Cashew Crunch
- Dark Chocolate Cherry
- Toasted Coconut Cacao

JJ Virgin's F-Glutamine Powder

L-Glutamine is an amino acid that is essential for the health of the immune system and the digestive tract. In the gut, it promotes the health and function of the mucosal cells for normal healing and repair. L-Glutamine also supports the optimal muscle growth and strength and has been shown to be particularly useful in helping to maintain muscle tissue, as it can be a substrate for protein synthesis and as an anabolic precursor for muscle growth.

So Delicious Dairy Free

http://sodeliciousdairyfree.com/products/

You can replace cow's milk with So Delicious® unsweetened coconut milk beverage, either as an ingredient in your protein smoothies or as a beverage in its own right. One cup contains just 50 calories and only 1 gram of sugar. It also offers medium-chain fatty acids, a healthy fat that your body easily burns for energy rather than stores.

If coconut milk isn't your thing, try So Delicious® unsweetened Almond Plus 5X Protein and my new favorite, Cashew Milk. So Delicious® also provides a delicious selection of no-sugar-added coconut milk ice cream and cultured coconut milk. One bite of these delicious treats and you'll wonder why you ever fell for cow's milk.

Kevita

Body Ecology Coco-Biotic

Body Ecology's Coco-Biotic helps restore and maintain your inner ecosystem to defend against disease-causing bacteria, viruses, yeast and other dangerous invaders. Fermented young coconut water brings you energy and vitality.

Wild Things Seafood & Steaks

www.WildThingsSeafood.com

I never knew that Chef-Ready Premium Quality Seafood, Grass Fed Beef and Lamb, Free Range Chicken and other fabulous clean and lean protein could be so affordable! For nearly 40 years, Wild Things Seafood parent and partner company West Coast Prime Meats have been providing premium protein to the most discriminating chefs at restaurants and luxury resorts across the United States. Now it is available direct to your kitchen. I have been impressed with everything Wild Things has sent me. Wild Things prices are consistently 20-40% lower than anywhere I have shopped online. I love sending gifts of Wild Things WOW to my friends and colleagues. You will love them too.

Hint Water

http://www.drinkhint.com

Hint Water evolved when San Francisco native Kara Goldin couldn't find a delicious, refreshing drink for her or her kids.

What she wanted was simple: no sweeteners, sugars, fancy but useless additives, or ingredients you can't pronounce. Just plain, delicious pure spring water with a splash of natural flavor. Sounds easy, right? It wasn't, which is why she created Hint Water.

When people tell me they don't like water or are trying to break their soda habit, I always recommend Hint Water in amazing flavors like raspberry-lime and strawberry-kiwi. Who says water has to be boring?

Infrared Sauna

http://www.sunlighten.com/?leadsource=JJVirgin

Sunlighten saunas use infrared heat instead of hot rocks or steam used in traditional saunas. Traditional saunas heat the air at extremely high temperatures which can make the experience unbearably hot and difficult to breathe. Because infrared heats the body directly instead of simply heating the air, infrared saunas are seven times more effective for detoxification. In a Sunlighten sauna, you will experience the deepest, most detoxifying sweat of your life.

Designs for Health Detox Packets

These packets are recommended as the starting point for detoxification programs, for anyone who needs regular detoxification support, or for those who want extra help before such things as dental amalgam removal or heavy metal chelation.

Blenders

Can't be beat for making smoothies! Powerful for those extra-thick-so-your spoon-stands-up-in-it ones that I like best! Yep, they are pricey, but **ORDER HERE** (https://www.vitamix.com/Shop/Blenders.aspx?COUPON=06-009044) to receive free shipping, a $25 value!

X-Iser

A second type of circulation, called your lymphatic system, helps fight infections and flush toxins out of your body. Lymph, also called interstitial fluid, is a watery clear fluid that carries waste to lymph nodes, which help filter that fluid. Especially when you detoxify, you want to keep that lymph continually flowing.

Sluggish lymphatic circulation means your immune system takes a hit and toxins build up. Keep your lymphatic circulating optimally by drinking plenty of filtered water, massage, yoga, and using a dry brush. You might also find a massage therapist who specializes in lymph drainage therapy.

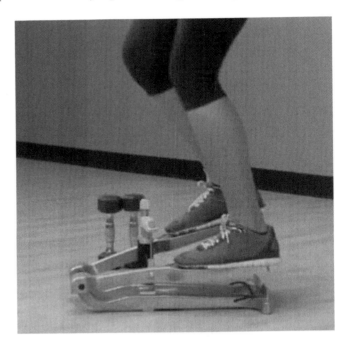

My favorite way to stimulate lymph is with the X-iser, a portable, easy-to-use, built-to-last little machine that (literally!) steps up circulation. You'll feel the burn and love the numerous benefits of getting a full-body, fat-blasting, detoxify-enhancing workout in just four minutes a day.

Made in the USA
Charleston, SC
27 February 2015